MERGING HEARTS

Understanding How to Bridge the Gap Between the Leader and the People

Dr. Haywood L. Parker

Orman Press • Lithonia, GA

MERGING HEARTS

UNDERSTANDING HOW TO BRIDGE THE GAP BETWEEN THE LEADER AND THE PEOPLE

DR. HAYWOOD L. PARKER

Copyright © 2001 by Orman Press

ISBN
1-891773-24-0
Printed in the United States of America

Orman Press, Inc.
4200 Sandy Lake Drive
Lithonia, GA 30038

———Acknowledgements———

This book is dedicated to the memory of my dear mother, Rosa L. Gaynor, who gave herself untiringly to helping me become all that she believed God had destined me to be. I will always be grateful for the level of prayer intercession that she engaged in for me personally, as well as for the church, Truth Tabernacle, which she helped me found and raise to be what it is today.

A special thanks goes to my good friend, Sharon Scott, who assisted me in the creation of this book and who attended classes that I taught in order to offer insights into my writing. I also owe a word of thanks to those who took my Saturday classes on leadership, through the Down East Christian Leadership Training Program, and who were forced to write and respond to materials that I had produced.

I do thank the Truth Tabernacle family for their support and prayers as I worked on this book. They are one of the most loving church families that a pastor can have. Much allegiance must be given to my dear friend, Leslie Takahashi-Morris, who has inspired my journey of exploring leadership as a discipline. It was through the Wildacres Leadership Program that our paths crossed, and we have walked together ever since.

Many thanks go to my spiritual father, Bishop Ralph L. Dennis, who took me in as a son and gave birth to renewed vision in my life. It has been through his encouragement that I regained the notion that there is life after death. Along with his support, I found strength and solace in Bishop Alfred Owens, who unselfishly afforded me opportunities to practice my leadership learning, while simultaneously offering words of wisdom about going on with life.

Last, but not least, I thank my family for their untiring support of what I do in the ministry. Many thanks to Pat, Lois and Lonnie for being good siblings who are also wonderful church members. I am indebted to the two most wonderful daughters, Shelayna and Stephanie, that a man can have.

And finally, to my most beautiful and precious wife, Wanda, who is a gift from heaven. She fought hard to keep me from giving up the calling of this book and pushed me to stay larger than life. Sometimes, I think she believes in me more than I do myself.

To God be the glory for the things He has done!

——Table of Contents——

———Foreword———

Bishop Haywood Parker has produced a scholarly and practical work dealing with the problems that we all face in shepherding congregations. For more than 40 years, I searched for some kind of working tool that would help close the space between what I envisioned and what the people understand. I've lamented over those I prepared to share leadership with me and ultimately entered their own sphere of leadership for those who just didn't seem to get the message. Bishop Parker has taken great pain to prepare the subject matter, by studying the problems and providing practical help. I highly recommend this text for every pastor and church worker. *Indeed, this book is a bridge over those perennial gaps.*

Bishop J. Delano Ellis, II
Presiding Bishop, The United Pentecostal Churches of Christ
President, Joint College of African-American Pentecostal Bishops

———Introduction———
The Keep-A-Gap Pentecostal Church

The Keep-A-Gap Pentecostal Church is a thriving and affluent church in the heart of Bridge Town, USA. The church is approximately 50 years old and has seen itself progress from a small storefront on the corner with 10 members to a large and beautiful edifice with approximately 1500 members. A wonderful person, whose pulpit ministry has attracted people by the dozens, pastors the church.

Recently, the pastor of Keep-A-Gap Church noticed that there was some discrepancy in what he was envisioning and in what the church was experiencing. The Holy Spirit led him to search the records and let the statistics authenticate his hunch regarding the discrepancy. The pastor was shocked by what he found.

The tithing pattern revealed that only about 47 percent were faithful tithers; the educational ministry revealed that only about 25 percent attended classes and schools; the workers' department revealed that 20 percent of the people were doing all of the work; a survey revealed that only about 15 percent of the people could articulate the pastor's vision and goals; a second survey revealed that there was something being stirred between those who are "new and gifted" and those who are "old and holding current positions."

Upon hearing the pastor's concerns, Elder Got the Pastor's Heart thought that this would be a great opportunity for the ministerial team of the church to help the pastor accomplish his vision. He took it upon himself to ask the elders and deacons to consider this as part of their next meeting. Upon sharing this with the pastor, it was also revealed that some of the elders and deacons were part of the percentage that was not in congruence with the pastor's vision, demands and needs.

Does the above scenario sound familiar? Can you identify on some level with the experience of this pastor? I suspect that many of us who are leaders and pastors have encountered times in our leadership when there seems to be some gap between what we desire to occur and what we see occurring. Many of the statistics in our local assembly reflect a widening gap between those who produce excellence and maximum participation, and those who are somewhat stagnant and produce minimally.

I have conducted several workshops in which I used this scenario as a tool for discussion. I asked the participants to read the scenario and then identify the leadership issues that they saw. It amazed me as to the large number of responses that were given, as well as to the diversity in the responses in terms of the identifiable issues. Some of the responses were as follows:

- *A lack of teaching on behalf of the leaders*

- *Lack of leader's ability to properly guide the congregation*

- *Accountability and responsibility issues*

- *Goals have not been revisited enough to perpetuate the history*

- *Lack of communication from pastor to the congregation*

- *There is a core group not being reached*

- *Deficit in operation*

- *Failure to transfer the vision*

- *Pastor had vision but the people did not*

- *Loss of enthusiasm or excitement among the congregation*

- *Question regarding the people being willing to be obedient*

- *The new members and the old members were in conflict*

- *Leaders were not fully doing their jobs*

- *Unclear values*

- *The name of the church fosters a spirit of division*

- *Nothing is wrong: this is a reality check of group functioning*

The Keep-a-Gap Church has issues that challenge many of us as leaders. If we gave this scenario to your church group, I am sure they would see issues that have not been listed. I think that what we all would agree on is that this church certainly has a multitude of concerns, but that they are no different than our own realities as church leaders. Many of us would love to know the solutions to closing the gap and eliminating some of the problems identified above. Herein lies the purpose of this book. *The intent of this book is to engage you and your leaders and/or followers into a dialogue about the issues you encounter in leadership, as well as to identify ways in which you can move toward empowering leadership to accomplish the vision of the church or organization.*

When we study the above scenario and try to ascertain what is happening, we will discover that there are several approaches to diagnosing what the problem may be. Our movement towards finding strategies and solutions is dependent upon which approach we take towards defining the problems.

As far as I am concerned, there are basically three approaches to this scenario. Firstly, we could deem the issues in this scenario as being primarily a "people problem" by attributing the gap to the lack of their obedience and proper response to the pastor's vision. Secondly, we could view the problem as being clearly a "pastor problem" in that there is something that the pastor is doing wrong to encounter such discrepancies between what he wants and has demanded, and what the people are producing. Thirdly, we could consider this from a "both/and" paradigm. This perspective would suggest that the issues in the scenario reflect both a pastoral problem as well as a people problem. It seems that the highest level of resolve will occur only if both the pastor and the people are willing to cooperatively own the problem as being theirs. Simultaneously, they must both then be willing to develop strategies and solutions that would bring the church to maximum effectiveness.

I do not claim to be the great solver of church problems, nor do I claim to have some "utopian church that is problem-free." As a matter of fact, it is quite the opposite, and thus arise the insights and motivation to write this book. I believe that there are leaders out there, such as myself, who are asking for someone to provide insights on church leadership and to explore ways to develop strategies and solutions that will strengthen our congregations. I know that there are many young pastors with tremendous potential to develop strong congregations but do not have a safe environment in which to ask questions and share their struggles around people problems and leadership development. The truth of the matter is that as long as we have people, we will always have people problems, or shall we more appropriately call them "people issues."

I invite you to journey with me as we explore what it means to lead and to examine different ways in which we can become effective leaders. We will begin with a reiteration of the commonalities in our work as leaders and with an identification of what I regard to be one of our major frustrations. Secondly, we will attempt to define terminology used in this book around the term "set gift" since it is my contention that this is a term now being generated in Christendom that is not familiar to all. Then, we will plunge into doing the real work of leadership. We will focus on what I deem as the starting point of moving an organization to its desired end. I am calling this beginning point, or the point where we will lead out from, *"VISION."*

After developing our understanding of vision and its relevance towards leadership, we will next examine the concept of leadership by attempting to move towards a proposed definition of the same. This definition will become the pivotal point from which we will continue our journey of struggling with leadership issues such as we encountered in the Keep-A-Gap scenario. Using our proposed model of leadership and contemporary issues we face daily as leaders, we will then brainstorm possible solutions and strategies that will enable us to close the gap between what we want as leaders and what we see occurring in our congregations.

Finally, we will conclude with a look at a slightly different twist to the widening of the gap concept. This has to do with the issue of understanding how to close the gap between the different generations that co-exist in our churches and organizations. Some strategies must be proposed to help decrease the span of separation that could potentially develop because we, as leaders, have only focused on the adult-to-adult issues in leadership. What will we do with the incoming generation that wants to become a part of the mainline but feel themselves excluded because of the discrepancies in new and old thinking? What will we do with the existing sector of the church who is threatened by the incoming group, and who refuses to embrace them holistically because they see them as marching to the beat of a different drummer?

May I suggest a paradigm or a lens through which we can maximize what we get from this reading? Many times, as leaders, we only deal with one dimension of our issues or problems. For example, we may focus on the behavior manifestations of problems and, thus, invest our energies around "Behavior Modification" theories, when actually the real force of the issue may not be the behavior. Sometimes, what people feel about their issue has more force and power than the resulting behavior that we see. In other words, underneath the symptomatic behavior is a symptomatic root feeling. Therefore, we must engage in both the processes of behavior and of feelings if we are going to foster conditions that will promote more effective leadership.

A third piece of this work is the one we gravitate to very easily. This is the exploration of the cognitive issues involved in the attempt to do leadership work together with others. It is really easy to release the majority of our emphasis on the cognitive dimension of our experiences. We have been trained by schools, universities, and other leadership programs, to approach our challenges through the analytical process. While I agree that this must be done, I am also convinced that there is much more work that has to be attended to. This work will be reflected in our leadership definition. The ways in which we must attend to this work will be based upon the issues that we deem important, as we attempt to troubleshoot our problems and concerns around leadership.

I have encountered a model from working with and supporting an organization called V.I.S.I.O.N.S (Vigorous Interventions In Ongoing Natural Settings) that I love to use. This organization proposes that the following model (see diagram on p. 16) be used as a way of dealing with organizational challenges around people working and existing together in a manner that is most conducive to the good of the people and the organization.

Cognitive

Ways People Think

Affective

Ways People Feel

Behavior

Ways People Act

As we explore this work together, I invite you to pay attention not only to what you are thinking and what you view as the "thinking dimension" of your challenges around leadership, but also to pay attention to the affective and behavioral components. I am really lifting up strongly the affective component because I believe that sometimes this is the most neglected area and becomes the place in which many of our leadership struggles are hidden or are deeply rooted. For a lot of people in our congregations, their response to us as leaders becomes wedged between what they think and what they feel. We must not only try to identify what they think and how our thinking may be different—and thus broaden the gap—but we must go a little deeper to determine if what they are feeling is increasing the gap even more.

Well, are you ready? I invite you now to take the next step and allow yourself to identify your current leadership struggles as you operate in your own context. Take a pencil and write down in the spaces provided, a response to the following questions.

1)   *How do I define leadership?*

2)   *What are some current leadership issues that I face?*

3)   *Is there a gap between what I envision as a leader and how I see the people around me functioning? If so, how do I describe this gap?*

——Chapter 1——
The Common Experience

Many leaders, if asked what is one of their most challenging problems in moving the church to where God has called it, would readily agree that it is basically that of mobilizing people. The challenge can be stated as that of "getting the mass of the congregation to function in a way that is congruent to what is in the heart of the set gift." Many times God has given us, as the set gifts of the house, revelations and visions that we are to accomplish. At the time in which it is birthed, we become excited and teem with joy. We gather energy and a momentum about what we have seen, what we have heard, and what we believe is the voice of God instructing us for the next piece of ministry. As we entrust this revelation to the hearts of the people, it seems sometimes as if only a minority or the same core group grasps what we relay and run with the baton. Sometimes this can become frustrating and lead to either an unexpected barrier in attaining our vision, or the premature death of many of our visions.

When the anointing of God comes upon us and births the vision in our hearts, or gives us a clear sense of direction for the next move of God in our local assemblies, it can be a very rewarding moment for the leader. As leaders, we know the price and the struggle that is involved in keeping a clear head and an undistracted mind in order to conceive the revelations of God. We have come to accept the reality that in our work, there will be many demands placed upon us, there will be many unexpected crises and interruptions, and there will be people problems that we must contend with on an ongoing basis. So when God can get through this entourage of events and penetrate our spirit, we are ready to celebrate the vision immediately. Sometimes, in the peak of our excitement, we forget the process that we must encounter in moving the vision from the heat of our excitement to the hearts of the people. Thus, we put the vision out to them with the anticipation that the people will grasp it in the same manner in which the vision grabbed us as leaders. When they do not seize it as we hoped, reality sets in and we experience a crushing of that which we thought would generate excitement.

Nothing is more frustrating to a pastor or leader, who is extremely zealous towards the work of the ministry, than to watch the vision crumble in the midst of the people. This is a very painful experience and has caused many leaders to lose their zest and their zeal for the work of God. The leader can love his assignment from God but resent the way in which people can allow their own selfishness and petty jealousies and personal idiosyncrasies to breed competition and division. This resentment, if not rechanneled and refocused, can lead the leader to the graveyard of dead visions. The epitaph will read once again, "Here lies another vision that the people destroyed." The leader must fight against this feeling of death. Hopefully, this book will offer insights as to how the leader can better empower the people so that the vision becomes a banner of victory rather than an epitaph on the tombstone of the dead.

We must be aware of possible pitfalls in doing leadership and caution ourselves regarding lessons learned from the past and from patterns in people's behavior. One pitfall is that we can be so ready for the end results of our vision that we literally forget the many times in which the same congregation has challenged what God has given us. The euphoria of the inception of the vision overrides the memory of yesterday's last expiring vision. We forgot how the people responded. Sometimes this is good because it prevents leaders from falling prey to the ambiance of people's functioning. Some leaders are so hurt from yesterday's memory that they resist going through the process of submitting their vision into the hands of the people again. They do not want to experience the pain of watching what happens to their God-given vision. They cry out, "We do not want this one to die also."

A second pitfall is that we can want 100 percent of the people on our side, doing exactly what we envision. This is an honorable goal but perhaps it falls short of reality. In his book on leadership, Dr. John Maxwell describes what he calls the Pareto principle. This principle of functioning among groups suggests that 20 percent of the people do 80 percent of the work. The problem with this dynamic is that the 20 percent eventually suffer burnout because they are repetitively carrying the load of the ministry in every event. The other problem is that human beings function in learned patterns and the 80 percent quickly learns and acquiesces to the 20 percent doing all of the work. The 80 percent become very comfortable with this process and never challenge themselves to do any different.

Eventually, the dynamic of the Pareto principle causes disharmony within the entire congregation and starts to drain the energy from the core of the group. This leads to what I call "Reverse Synergism." Synergism suggests that the "whole is greater than the sum of its parts" and that the energy released is a synergetic kind of energy on which the whole group thrives because it is larger than the group. Reverse Synergism would suggest that "the whole is less than the sum of its parts." This implies that the negative dynamic occurring due to the sense of inequity in the group is withdrawing unseen energy from the group. As a result, the group is functioning beneath its maximum capacity.

The negative energy arises from the fact that "interdependency" is a strong group value. Each member of a group values the relationship that is shared with the other members in the group and the interrelatedness of their functioning. Watching one person contribute to the whole of the organization should cause others to also make contributions in an equivalent or more excellent manner. However, we know that it does not always happen like this. Sometimes, watching one or more persons fail to make a contribution to the whole can cause others, out of sheer frustration, to lose motivation for contribution. Leaders, in particular, have to guard against this phenomenon in a way in which it can have an impact on them, as well as on the group's functioning.

All throughout the Scriptures, we can trace this dynamic occurring in a group context, that caused some level of dissension and breakdown in expectations. Simultaneously, we can trace the effect of this disparity in functioning between the leader and the people. Such disparity also effects the leader's ability to tenaciously hold to the vision at hand.

First, we see Moses in the Old Testament, who had the enormous task of leading the Israelites from Egypt to Canaan land. In a sense, Moses is a prototype of our modern day pastor who was given a mega-church to lead. His challenge, in this leadership role, foreshadowed almost every possible issue that we as leaders face today as we attempt to mobilize people to embrace the vision of our local assemblies. His response to this group of people resounds loudly in the ears of many leaders—who continue to walk on the edge between leading with hope and resigning to frustration—as they try to reach the ultimate place of fulfilling their God-given vision.

No place in the Bible is this scenario more eloquently and descriptively spoken of than that given by Stephen, the great deacon of the early church, who was filled with the Holy Ghost and power, in the Book of Acts, Chapter 7. As Stephen was offering his defense for the faith, and as he understood the accusations that he had blasphemed God and Moses, he revisited the annals of time and unveiled to his accusers the vision concerning God, Abraham, Moses and Jesus Christ.

Concerning Moses, Stephen rehearses how God chose Moses as a child and then, at the ripe age of 80, appears to him in a theophanic experience. An angel speaks to Moses out of a burning bush which cannot be consumed and informs him that he has been chosen by the Almighty to go down to Egypt and set God's people free from the hand of Pharaoh. After a brief interlude of questioning the revelation given to him and doubting his own abilities to accomplish this task, Moses embarks upon the journey and succeeds in getting the people released from slavery in Egypt. Little did he know that the emancipation of the people was only a small part of his biggest challenge. The greatest challenges were ahead of him because now he had to transition the people from Egypt to Canaan. Such transition would involve the art of leading them to both a change of thinking and of locale. Stephen thus calls him, implicitly, the pastor of the church in the wilderness. In Acts 7:38-39 it reads:

This is he, that was in the church in the wilderness
with the angel which spake to him in the mount Sina,
and with our fathers: who received the lively oracles to
give unto us: To whom our fathers would not obey, but
thrust him from them, and in their hearts turned back
again into Egypt.

Within this text and contextual environment, we identify the
leadership challenge that lies at the heart of this book. Pastor
Moses, as the set gift of the church in the wilderness, is given
an assignment and a vision by the Almighty, but the people
refused to obey him and preferred to turn back towards Egypt,
rather than march to their freedom. The dynamics of their
experience reveals how the negative synergy, as a result of the
actions of some of the people, caused more of those who
would have ordinarily followed willingly, to resist the leadership of Moses and become part of the callousness of the masses.

From our understanding of the remainder of this story,
according to the Book of Deuteronomy, we know that Moses
became so vexed and frustrated by the people's continual
rebellion and resistance to his leadership, that he falls short of
entering the total promise of God. Somehow, Moses could
never mobilize the people to reach 100 percent unity and to
pool their energies collectively to create a synergistic environment that would have fostered the success of the whole congregation. He continued to experience a breakdown in leader-

ship from Aaron, his second man in charge, to the team sur-
rounding him and Aaron, and down to the bottom level of laity
support. What a challenge Moses had. Many times, I wonder
how any leader could have stood in the midst of such extreme
adversity.

But what do we do as leaders when, in a microcosmic manner, we encounter the same dynamics as Moses did while trying to bring people to the place of their freedom in God?
What do we do when our next line of leadership gravitates
toward the mass of the people and empowers their rebellion
against us as set gifts? What do we do when the people collectively join forces and overtly cry against our leadership,
creating negative synergism in the congregation? What do we
do?

I am not certain of all the answers, but this book will make
a strong attempt to help us think about this issue. One of the
places I would suggest we turn for solace is to that of Jesus
Christ, the anti-type of Moses and the highest order of humanity that we can examine. We should be able to look at how He
led His congregation from the shores of the world to the gates
of the church. As we examine the dynamics of his experience,
we see that he encountered the same kind of occurrences as
Pastor Moses. It makes one think that there is some kind of
ubiquitous notion in leading people which suggests that the
clearest pattern of leadership contains a challenging course
that is, at best, swampy, oscillating and non-linear.

The Notion of Leadership

As we try to examine the notion of what leadership looks like, some would say that it should be neat and linear.

We would like to believe that

Leadership is a Straight Line

The Starting Point

However, what we find in actuality is that
Leadership Oscillates between Highs and Lows

The Starting Point

and . . .
Is Quite A Swampy Area

Leadership in the Swamp is Messy and Chaotic

Our understanding of Jesus' leadership stems from his functioning with the twelve disciples as his core leadership team,
along with the seventy that he chose on the next level, and
finally down to the multitude he tried to lead. What we see is
that even with his uniqueness and restrictions within the
boundaries of humanity, Jesus encountered much frustration
and many of the same leadership challenges as Moses. Many
times, as He tried to convey the vision to his leadership team,
He found himself being the only one grasping the revelation
and the vision of his Father. Thus, He had to challenge the
behaviors of his group because they acted upon their interpretation of what he said, and for the most part, there was a major
discrepancy between His revelation and their interpretation.

What became even more frustrating to Jesus was the manner in which the actions of one or more of the disciples would
trigger the functioning of the others and cause the entire group
to default.

Jesus discovered that each one of his disciples responded
differently to his teachings and that there was a type of negative synergism operating when they all relied on one leader.
Even at his best, Jesus died without them having a full grasp
of what he was teaching because of the dynamics of mobilizing the entire group to follow him.

Chapter 2
Understanding the Term "Set Gift"

The term "set gift" is a fairly new term for me. I've been in the church nearly all of my life and had never even heard the term until recently. This represents almost four decades of growing up in the church with basically using the terminology of "the Pastor" of the church. Let me add an immediate disclaimer: I am not suggesting at all that we discontinue the use of this term or that there is something inherently wrong with this language—such a position would be anti-biblical. What I am suggesting, however, is that the way in which we view our leaders in our churches will have an impact on the manner in which we reverence and respect their positions. Herein lies my gravitation towards the term "set gift."

The word "set," according to Webster, has multiple meanings. What I saw in common with most of the definitions is that the word implies to place, to arrange, to appoint or to fix for some reason or for some purpose. In other words, the definition implies that when one sets something in place, it is done with a clear motive or a clear end in mind.

The notion of "set gift" can actually be traced from our Old Testament understanding to the gleanings that we gain from the New Testament. In Old Testament theology, we encounter the idea of "chosenness" as we see how God operated in His dealings with mankind. The idea of chosenness suggests that God chooses from among His creation, a person or persons to accomplish a certain task, which He has in His heart. Examples of this would be the choosing of Abraham as the

progenitor of faith, Moses as the liberator from Egyptian slavery, or Joseph as the liaison between Egypt and Israel. In all
of these examples, God chose and identified the person to
lead, and then providentially arranged their lives to execute
His desires. It is in these stories regarding our Old Testament
leaders that we get our first glimpse of how God chooses and
then, in the simplest sense of the word, "sets" persons in a
strategic place to carry out a particular function.

In a broader context, Jeremiah the prophet sees this occurrence happening in the way in which God identified shepherds
and prophets to oversee His people during their rebellious
days against the Lord God of Israel. Hence, we hint at the
leadership challenge of the set gift once again. Jeremiah's
assurance to the people was that in spite of their sinfulness and
blatant rebellion, God still loved and cared for them. God had
a plan in His heart whereby they could become all that He had
chosen them to be. Part of that plan involved proper leadership and the identification of someone to mobilize the people
enough to lead them towards the Creator's desires for them.
Thus Jeremiah declared the promise of the Lord: *"And I will
give you pastors according to mine heart, which shall feed
you with knowledge and understanding"* *(Jeremiah 3:15,
emphasis added).* God tells Jeremiah that He would give or
set leaders in place to direct the people into His promise.

As we journey towards the gleanings in the New Testament,
we get our best understanding of the notion of set gift from
Paul the Apostle. According to Paul's understanding of the
church, in Ephesians 4, Jesus Christ descended into the grave
and ascended after three days. It was immediately following
his ascension that Jesus gave gifts unto the church (or gave
five ministries to the Body of Christ for a specific purpose).

The Scripture says, "...when He ascended up on high, He led captivity captive, and gave gifts unto men.... And he gave some, apostles; and some, prophets; and some, evangelists; and some, pastors and teachers" (Ephesians 4:8, 11).

Paul writes to the church at Corinth and again says, "And God hath set some in the church, first apostles, secondarily prophets, thirdly teachers, after that miracles, then gifts of healings, helps, governments, diversities of tongues" (1 Corinthians 12:28).

The idea is that God dispenses, establishes and appoints the offices and the gifts of the church as He sees necessary. God placed, or set, the gifts to bring about His desired purpose for His church. If we correlate Ephesians 4 with 1 Corinthians 12, we see first that the gifts of the apostle, prophet and teacher are listed in the same order in both texts. Therefore, if Paul uses the term "set" in 1 Corinthians 12, then it would follow logically that the term must also be applicable to Ephesians 4. If this is true regarding the first three gifts of Ephesians 4, then it must also follow for the latter two of the pastor and the evangelist.

Again I would like to emphasize the difference in how I am using the term "set gift" versus just the term "pastor." When the term "pastor" is used, it could refer to any and all of the ways in which one becomes the pastor of a church. For some, this is by divine appointment; for others, it is by a political process of voting; for others, it is by inheritance or succession; and for others, it is by self-appointment. My challenge in using the term "set gift" is to transcend the ways in which we become "pastor" and focus on the ultimate understanding of "who made us pastor." I believe that ultimately God should choose and set us forth as pastors. After all, the gifts belong to Him, and he can dispense them as He chooses and to whom he chooses.

According to Ephesians 4:12-13, ministry gifts are given primarily for three purposes:

> For the perfecting of the saints, for the work of the ministry, for the edifying of the body of Christ: Till we all come in the unity of the faith, and of the knowledge of the Son of God, unto a perfect man, unto the measure of the stature of the fullness of Christ.

To further clarify the term "set," we can think of the writing in Acts 20:28 where Peter says, "...and to all the flock, over which the Holy Ghost hath made you overseers, to feed the church of God, which he hath purchased with his own blood." Here we see the preciousness of the church of God and the value of it to God Himself. God loved His church enough to purchase it with his own blood, which he shed at Calvary. In other words, He gave his life and allowed himself to pay the ultimate price for his church. Greater love has no man than to lay down his life for his brothers. What blesses me about this process is that God paid the price to buy His church, and then skillfully and carefully designed a process whereby the church would mature and become His bride. Then He himself anointed and appointed leaders to oversee and feed the people of his church.

According to the Gospel writers, God handpicked the first twelve leaders of the church. When He chose them, they were mere humans with multiple sins and blooming failures in their lives. Peter, James and John were fishermen who were not catching fish after fishing all night; Matthew (or Levi), the tax collector, was ripping off the people by charging an excess for taxes; Judas was the one who betrayed Him; and Peter was the one who denied Him publicly. Yet God chose these men as servants to raise up and anoint—to reorder their lives for the kingdom of God and for the church of God. He kept working with them until they were ready to be released to oversee the church of God. It was Peter, the one who seemed to have failed Him the most, that stood up on the day of Pentecost as God's ambassador and explained to the listeners what God was establishing in their midst (see Acts 2:14-36).

It was Paul, the great killer of the Christians—whom God appointed as the greatest apostle ever—who wrote practically half of the New Testament. God chose him and changed his life on the road to Damascus. Paul declares that the love of Christ constrains us to live unto him; therefore, if any man be in Christ, he is an ambassador for Christ (see 2 Corinthians 5:14-20). Paul believed that God set him in the church to be an apostle, and thus declared this in many of his letters. To the church at Ephesus he writes, "Paul, an apostle of Jesus Christ by the will of God, to the saints which are at Ephesus..." (Ephesians 1:1). He identified himself as having been chosen by God. The term "apostle" comes from the word meaning "one who is sent." Paul was set forth and sent by God.

This is the understanding that is perpetuated in the term "set gift" of the church or "set gift" of the house. Being the "set gift" in the house of the Lord is a matter that cannot be taken lightly. It is a serious assignment if we can view it from an eternal perspective, as God does. The set gift is the man or woman whom God Himself has entrusted with the task of leading His people in such a wholesome, effective and powerful way that the church will be fully equipped to bring forth the kingdom of God in the realm of the earth. In order for this task to be accomplished, the set gift must continually feed the flock with knowledge and understanding. This continual and sometimes grueling process can usually help distinguish between those pastors who have been set in place by God and those who put themselves into place. Unless the Spirit of the Lord dwells within and upon the set gift and the anointing has been released for a particular assignment, it can be expected that the tenure of the non-anointed and non-appointed will be short-lived. Even those who have been divinely appointed and set by God, fight to stay within the confines of the calling without throwing in the towel because of negative synergism and painful leadership experiences.

The Ecclesia (the church) is the called out body whom God has chosen to work through to manifest His power and glory in the earth. Therefore, it is incumbent that a system of government be set in place for the operation, the continued movement and the empowerment of the church. It is quite necessary that the masses receive those whom the Lord has sent and set, and trust them to lead the congregation in the way that God would have them go. The responsibility then lies not only with the masses to follow, but also with the "set gift" to lead in a manner that maximizes the people's desire to follow in a manner which is consistent with the vision given by God.

———Chapter 3———
Do You See What I See?
Beginning with Vision

As we move towards our goal of exploring ways to bridge the gap between what is in the heart of the set gift and the functioning of the people, we must determine the appropriate place to begin. Do we start with the people, or do we start with the set gift? Do we look outward towards other models of ministry that we can duplicate and mimic, or do we search the soul of the ministry internally to find the energy, which lies dormant? Do we begin with attacking behavior patterns, or do we search for the core philosophical principles upon which our organization is based? Do we inquire of others who seem to possess intellectual expertise around organizational strategies, or do we ask of the Omniscient regarding His revelations of creation for our local assembly? All of these are legitimate questions. They are all strong contenders for ways to discover how to empower our assembly, and thus it would be inappropriate to pitch them against each other in an "either/or" paradigm. It is probably more helpful to develop a "both/and" paradigm in which we see substantive help emerging from all the above resources.

It is the contention of this book, however, that while all must be examined and explored, the more appropriate and expedient approach is to begin with the heart of the set gift. This is an intentional strategy underlying the thinking of this book because so many leaders, in my opinion, shift blame externally and never examine the impact of their own functioning upon the dynamic of the organization. The truth of the matter is that unless the one chosen as leader is clear about the assignment, the purpose, the revelation and the vision, then the people's functioning will always be substandard and difficult.

In order for people to follow with minimum challenges, they must be given a proper understanding of the plan and strategies for accomplishing the same. Any cloudiness and confusion around the vision of the leader or around organizational vision creates conditions that will lessen the opportunity for the success of the organization itself. There is a Christmas song we sing called "Drummer Boy" that echoes through my mind as I write this chapter. The first line of the song is so synchronous with what I want to say. The words are, "Said the shepherd boy to the little lamb, do you see what I see?" I am convinced that we can be in the same field with people and they never see the star that bid us come to a new place. Way up in the sky, we as leaders can see dreams and revelations to accomplish the work of God, while those around us never get it. How do we translate the power of what we see into their spirits?

There is a proverb that I admire and esteem as having evolving truths. I say this because each time I study the proverb, it seems as if I glean other elements of truth, which just jump out of the saying. The proverb is simple: *"WHERE THERE IS NO VISION, THE PEOPLE PERISH"* (Proverbs 29:18, *emphasis added*). As one begins to exegete this verse and to focus on the semantic understanding of the words "vision" and "perish," it will become clear that there are other ways to phrase this sentence. I am particularly driven to embrace the Revised Standard Version (RSV) translation of this proverb, which states, "Where there is no prophecy, the people cast off restraint." Another translation, the New Century Version, says, "Where there is no word from God, people are uncontrolled."

The wisdom writer clearly suggests that as we try to assess and explain the behaviors and the functioning of the people, we must begin with the revelation by which the people are operating. If there is no clear revelation or clear word from the Lord or no prophecy in the local assembly, of God's declared order and intent, then the people will not understand the parameters by which they must operate. Herein lies the issue of canonicity.

A canon is a measure or a rule or a standard. The canonization process offers the people a law or a guide, which becomes the standard of operation. In the Old Testament, the prophetic revelations of Moses became the canon of the children of Israel. Based upon Moses' revelation of what God wanted and required of them, the church in the wilderness was able to emerge as a monotheistic organization whose sole purpose was to obey God's commandments as they traveled toward their destiny in Canaan. Whenever the people lost sight or focus of the words of Moses or questioned the authority and authenticity of his word, they literally cast off restraints and operated outside of the boundaries by which they originally defined themselves.

The wisdom writer gleans from this understanding and thus uses the word "perish." In the Hebrew transliteration of this word, we discover the root word "para," which means to "let go." When the vision of the leader is lost or is not clearly stated and defined, or becomes part of the muddiness of the swamp, the tendency of people is to lean towards a natural propensity of chaos. They will let go of the abstract theoretical concepts of what they remember about the vision in order to search for something more concrete and defined. Herein lies my presumption that as the organization or church, in this case, seeks to redefine itself, it must start with the basic question of "Who are we?" and "Why are we formed?"

Margaret Wheatley, in her book *A Simpler Way*, suggests the following about organizations, which I think have relevance in the context of my writings. She states that "every organization calls itself into being as a belief that something more can be accomplished by joining with others. At the heart of every organization is a self reaching out to new possibilities." Wheatley's thinking would suggest that we organize as a church order to enhance the quality of our experience with God, to make our lives more purposeful through relationship and to affirm and enrich our identity as partners in our faith. Out of this seed of organizing, there emerges an identity that is trying to be expressed. According to Wheatley, people fall in love with this identity and they connect to the founding vision.

Out of this founding vision, which started first with the leader, or the set gift, and then became a shared vision of the people, there arises a passion to help the entire organization become what it was birthed to be. The passion becomes the catalyst for the synergetic functioning of the people. The passion becomes the seedbed of accomplishments and fulfillment. The passion becomes the fervor to execute that which has been conceived in the mind and brought forth into reality. Wheatly also suggests that we must be careful not to allow our passion to mutate into procedures and thus be about the business of institutionalizing the thing that keeps us alive. When this happens, we make policies, procedures, rules and laws as a means of trying to motivate people to do what passion once empowered them to do. The alpha experience gets lost in the quagmire of the journey, and thus, the people lose their way.

When people lose sight of the founding vision, they also experience a dampening of the fire by which they are warmed. This warmth is the energy that holds them together in the organization and which expands their ability to give birth to new and emerging ideas. This warmth keeps the church new, keeps the people fresh and attracts others to become part of an evolving system. So when the fire dies, the vision must be revisited and understood again.

Before we attempt to give a definitive position on the term "vision," let me share an experience of mine that affected the functioning of the congregation I pastor. There was a difficult season in ministry during which I was trying to lead people to accomplish a work for God, when indeed my own sense of vision and my own fire and passion had dwindled to practically nothing. I remember this experience just like it was yesterday.

For approximately fifteen years, I was pastor of a congregation that I had the pleasure of founding under the auspices of the Holy Spirit in May 1980. For years, my spouse and I worked together to build this church to a place in which the people enjoyed their encounter with the presence of God through worship and the teachings of the word. The church was pretty successful for a small town environment and had come to a high degree of respectability in the city. I had managed to matriculate through the educational environment and had received a BS degree, a Master of Divinity degree and a Doctorate in Adult Education from major universities. I simultaneously had become heavily involved in civic activities and ministerial events in the community. Therefore, the church had embraced a leader who was considered in the eyes of many to be quite successful and who was publicly acknowledged as a leader in the community.

Then the big day happened. It was a day analogous in my mind, on a minute and microcosmic level, to "D" day for the USA when Pearl Harbor was bombed or to the Dark Thursday in 1929 when the Stock Market crashed to its lowest ever. I know some of you may struggle with my analogy, but until you have fallen from public accolades of celebrating your success to public crucifixion of celebrating your fall, it would be difficult for you to identify with my analogy. But on the big day, my spouse left me and my marriage ended up in divorce. In another book, I will share my theological struggles and lessons learned from this horrific experience. For the purposes of this discussion, it is only significant to know that this experience became part of a series of events that practically destroyed any sense of vision I had for leading God's people, along with dampening the passion for accomplishing any work of the Lord.

Yet, I had to find the inner strength to keep going and to honor the congregation who said, "In spite of your failure, we still want you to lead us." They took this position because as they analyzed the facts in the case, they could not hold me hostage for something over which I had no control. I am grateful to them for this, but I cannot begin to explain the leadership challenges that emerged as I attempted to lead them during this season. The greatest challenge that I encountered had to do with vision and trying to lead people when my own vision had faded into the cloud of despair. I found myself with no motivation to lead and no desire to do anything except what was necessary. It was as if I could not see any further than my pain, and I had come to believe that life was really over.

About two years later, I went to a three-day workshop with my spiritual father, Bishop Ralph Dennis, from Baltimore, Md. It was during this workshop that I encountered an experience with the Holy Spirit which renewed my vision and my fervor for doing the work of the ministry. What my father shared in those sessions brought life to my spirit; and my eyes seemed as if they were opened again. I cried and repented because I had walked for the last two years in practical darkness—oblivious to the need to challenge my congregation to maximize what God had told us to do. I wept and sobbed because I was grateful that God loved me enough to pour healing oil into my wound and stir up my leadership potential again.

This is what my father shared. He drew the following diagram and then talked about the level of vision that some of us were encountering, as well as preached emphatically about the level of vision required to do successful ministry.

Functioning with a view of the big picture

Functioning with a larger view of what God wants but not looking at the big picture

Functioning with little vision; just enough to keep the group intact

Functioning with no vision except past remnants of what you know to do

I am still amazed as to the power of the Holy Spirit to regenerate the life in the spirit of the leader to accomplish what God has purposed for that leader to do. In spite of the ways in which we allow circumstances, challenging situations and even failures to place a cloud of darkness over our eyes and to silence our desire to lead people to the place God has called us, there is still resurrection power in the Holy Spirit. The same Spirit that quickened Jesus in the grave can quicken our crushed, wounded and sometimes dead spirits to see God again, afresh. It is similar to the experience of

Hagar in the 16th Chapter of Genesis.

Sarah and Abraham wounded Hagar, and her spirit was crushed and bruised. In her fear and pain, Hagar fled to the desert in order to avoid being mistreated by Sarah. The Scripture declares, "The angel of the Lord found Hagar near a spring in the desert; And he said, 'Hagar, servant of Sarah, where have you come from, and where are you going?'" (Gen. 16:7, 8). The angel then revealed to her what her destiny would be, as well as the fact that she was currently with child. He showed her vision. Hagar declared, after being overwhelmed by the theophanic revelation of God, his name is Jehovah-Roi, being interpreted, "You are the God who sees me."

Beloved, I am convinced that my experience is analogous to that of Sarah and could be analogous to yours too. I know that there are many leaders who have been so hurt and so wounded by either life's experiences and/or the people they serve, that they feel the vision has been annulled or is expiring even as they read this book. Just as the Holy Spirit revitalized the vision in me, He will do the same for you. God touched me at that meeting with my father, and He showed me that the reason my church was not prospering and experiencing growth was due to improper leadership. I was trying to lead people when my vision was at its lowest and weakest point.

As a matter of fact, what became clear to me in subsequent years was that I was not following the leading of the Spirit to take the congregation to its desired place. Actually, I was being led by the voice of pain and suffering. I realized that pain had become my "surrogate Holy Spirit." Whatever my pain told me, I had internalized, and had come to believe that my ability to accomplish the vision was over and that people would no longer follow me. I saw all the symptoms of rebellion and looseness. I saw people being nonchalant and seemingly having no motivation. Yet something strange occurred to me even though I did not penetrate the understanding of it: the people were still intact, still coming to church Sunday after Sunday, and still following me. What was this about?

It was then that the Holy Spirit showed me that I was the real deterrent to the vision. I had sunk to practically a zero level of vision. I could see no further than yesterday. I was functioning mechanically and operating out of the remnants of yesterday's vision. You and I both know that yesterday's vision will sustain one until clarity comes. But we also know that yesterday's vision is like a car running on empty—eventually it will run out of gas and stall. I had run out of gas, and the car had stalled.

In the midst of my tank being empty and stuck in the grieving process, I heard the Holy Spirit speak to me again during my *early morning prayer hours*. He spoke concerning how my grief was blinding my ability to hear Him tell me about how to get to the next level of doing ministry. He, the Holy Spirit, said: "You are so busy grieving that you cannot see where I am trying to take you. You are just like my disciples when I was trying to shift them to the next dimension of the work they had to accomplish. They were so encumbered with grieving over my leaving them, that they missed entirely what I was training them to do."

In the 14th through the 16th Chapters of the Gospel of John, Jesus gives a discourse to his disciples on his departure from them. He tells them that he must leave them and go the place of his death, burial and resurrection. He reminds them that they had only a little while to remain with Him, and then he would go to the place that the Father had prepared. These words pierced their very soul and saturated their hearts with grief. Jesus tells them, "Let not your hearts be troubled" (John 14:1). He further tells them that the time is coming when their grief will be turned into joy. I love the analogy that He uses in John 16:21:

> A woman giving birth to a child has pain because her time has come; but when her baby is born she forgets the anguish because of her joy that a child is born into the world. So with you: Now is your time of grief, but I will see you again and you will rejoice and no one will take away your joy.

Jesus revealed to his disciples, and he personally revealed this word to me, that the unfolding of the next dimension of the vision will produce a joy that will shift into perspective the pain that they were experiencing. The next dimension of the vision will reflect light on the relationship between "the child born out of suffering" and "the pain required to give birth." In order for me to grasp this, I had to challenge myself to get beyond the pain of failure and push beyond the grief, and ask God what is the next part of the vision. Where do I go from this place of death? What are the possibilities of resurrection, and where would resurrection take me to?

When my father shared the four-dimensional view of vision, the Holy Ghost filled my tank up again and the grieving process quickly subsided. All of a sudden, it was like a fire exploded in me. The scales fell from my eyes, and I could see clearly again. I felt like Hagar in the wilderness. Right in my desert experience, God revealed Himself and revived my vision, along with direction to accomplish the same. I started seeing the big picture. The big picture (macro vision) was about God and His purpose. It was about the kingdom of God and the ways in which God has anointed us to accomplish His purposes. The big picture was hidden under the layers and layers of pain. The smaller picture (micro vision) of mere survival had emerged as the guiding force. But now I found myself resisting a mere survivalist mentality. I started experiencing a kinetic energy to get on with living and the work of the ministry. I felt the force in me to reach again for the higher calling and the greater vision.

I can almost hear the subconscious voice of the readers saying, "I celebrate the experience of the writer and the fact that the Holy Spirit spoke to him." The question on the table for us is, How do we ascend or progress from zero vision to macro vision, especially if our pain dictates our path and yesterday's vision is the governor of our soul? How do we progress to the next level of vision if our faith in the productivity level of our congregation or organization is at a minimum? How do we muster up the energy to soar again to the ultimate heights of vision if the discrepancy between what we once saw occurring in leadership is a far cry from what we now see?

In my estimation, this is where the power of understanding vision comes in. Vision is an essential element and is extremely vital to the revival, to the sustenance, and to the longevity of any church, organization, or group entity. It is equally as important to the individuals doing the work of an organization. As leaders, we cannot be about the business of creating shared vision if our own vision and direction has reached a zero level of existence. Therefore, let us explore more intensely this issue of vision and its power towards our ultimate goal of successfully leading an organization to accomplish its purpose and destiny.

I realize that as I have used the term "vision" thus far, I have operated under the assumption that the reader brings his or her own definition into the experience of grappling with the thesis of the writer. I do think it would be helpful, however, to make an attempt to bring some clarity around my use of the word "vision."

The pivotal question for the purposes of this discussion is to inquire about "what vision is." Many attempts have been given to define this term, and I am sure that my notion of vision is no different than what you as a reader have already encountered and use as your definition. For example, a look in Webster's dictionary would simply give a definition that "vision is the act or power of imagination, or a mode of seeing or conceiving, or an unusual discernment or foresight." This definition comes far short of tapping into the kind of thinking that is necessary to lead a group of people into some collective action or to some desired outcome. It leaves too many questions to be reckoned with: What is the source of this imagination? Imagination for what? What are we trying to see?

One of the best definitions of vision that I have come across is that of George Barna's, in his book *The Power of Vision*. He states his definition in the context of doing ministry. According to Barna, "vision is a clear mental image of a preferable future imparted by God to His chosen servants and is based upon an accurate understanding of God, self and circumstances." The aspect of this definition, which highly resonates with my contention around vision, is that God imparts vision to His chosen servants. The nature of the work, which we must undertake as church leaders, must be birthed through the Holy Spirit into our spirits. Secondly, that which has been birthed must then be brought into the focus of our minds so that we have a clear mental image of what God has shown us through the Spirit. Thirdly, this clear image should project into our minds and our future. We should begin seeing projections of our work and ministry beyond its yesterday and today.

This is where the power of the Holy Spirit comes in. The writer of Hebrews 4:12 suggests that the word of God divides asunder soul and spirit. I believe that through the means of the Spirit, the Lord sends a word to our human spirit via vision. He causes this word to separate our soul from our spirit. He then fills the spirit with His desires and purposes, while simultaneously sanctifying the soul from its pain, bitterness, blindness and imprisonment. Then, He brings the soul back up under the authority of the spirit in a way that both soul and spirit are at one in their capacity to produce the vision and engage in the work of ministry. As a result, we are now able to see clearly what God is telling us about our future and the future of the ministry.

Herein lies the connection to my own stab at the definition of vision. For me, vision is a clear revelation and a clear picture of a desired outcome, birthed in us by the Holy Spirit. It consists of an unveiling of the heart of God regarding a specific purpose for a person or group of persons. This unveiling simultaneously entails the painting of a picture in the mind and spirit of the leader as to what that outcome looks and feels like.

There are three clear factors involved in this birthing of the vision in the heart of the leader:

1.   VISION IMPLIES RELATIONSHIP

The proposed definition operates out of the assumption that vision emanates from God as the great giver of all vision. Therefore, ascertaining this vision would require and demand that one spend time in the presence of God in order to become impregnated with the mind of God. It is similar to the intimacy between a man and his wife. The longer they spend time in the presence of each other, the easier it is for them to conceive the seeds that will produce their children. Simultaneously, this intimacy creates the capacity for them to give birth to a oneness in their own relationship so that they can share each other's heartbeat and mind very easily. So it is with God. The more we spend time in worship, in prayer and in just being with Him, the easier it will be for us to conceive the next part of the vision.

2.   VISION IMPLIES REVELATION

Vision implies that God has chosen to disclose Himself to us as leaders. As humans, we do not possess the capacity to unveil God and to know Him unless He chooses to reveal Himself. Therefore, when we become pregnant, or filled with vision, it is to be celebrated because God has chosen to show us how to properly lead His people and has given us the necessary revelation to do so. As leaders, we know that it is very difficult to just create things to do that will empower the organization or move the church to its next level.

Many leaders resort to duplicating popular ministries or

replicating the spirit of some great charismatic leader in trying to produce vision. As a result, they give birth to many "bastard visions." Bastard visions are visions without proper fathers and, therefore, without proper rearing, because the ones who released the seed do not even know that they gave birth to this vision and have no continual relationship with the vision. However, when God is the Father of the vision and He gives revelation to the leader, He will also become an active father in nurturing and providing for the vision that He gave birth to.

3.   VISION IMPLIES REHEARSAL

An underlying assumption of the writer is that the leader will come to a place to know what is God-given vision versus vision merely birthed out of duplication. Leaders who have wrestled with God and with pain will indulge in the process of revisiting yesterday's vision and yesteryear's experiences in order to determine what worked and what did not. They will grapple with the reasons and the causes of failure and/or success. This experience will get translated into their ability to grasp the next horizon of the vision being birthed in them. It is similar to a rehearsal for a big theatrical production. The repertoire producing the production will have rehearsed enough that they know what to change, to edit, to let go of and what to let die. As a result, they give birth to maximum performance.

Vision is not just about doing something or accomplishing a thing. It is quite multifaceted and must be carefully unfolded in order for the leader to be gripped by that which will sustain him/her during the challenges around execution of the vision. Therefore, we must press further to suggest that vision is a revelation and an understanding of what one is to "be," along with a view of what one is doing as he/she is "being." The pivotal point of emergence for this definition is seeing vision as a focus on being rather than just doing. Until leaders know what they are to be, I suspect that they will always struggle with knowing what they are to do.

Jesus made this point very plain to his disciples when he called them to follow him as he carried out the assignment given to him by his Father. In Mark 3:13-15 the writer states:

> Jesus went up on a mountainside and called to him those he wanted, and they came to him. He appointed twelve—designating them apostles—that they might **_be with him_** and that he might send them out to preach and to have authority to drive out demons. (*Emphasis added*)

I am convinced that until our vision is undergirded by a revelation of being what we have been called to be, we will continue to experience frustration around executing it and will continue to witness the premature death of many of our visions.

Vision also involves looking ahead with a desired end in mind. When God impregnates you with vision, he shows you the end. Vision is like the finished product of something you are about to produce. It is out of this revelation of the finished product that purpose is conceived and destiny is believed. It is also out of this revelation of the end that passion is generated to accomplish what God has shown you down the road. The passion becomes (1) the impetus for motivation and (2) the foundation for the discipline necessary to bring forth the vision.

When God impregnates you with vision, you see things that no one else sees. I'm reminded of a song that the church of yesterday used to sing. The words were, "I'm gonna run on to see what the end's gonna be." It is probably safe to assume that the songwriter had some idea of what he/she wanted or expected the end to look like. When we have a view of the end in mind, it empowers us to diagnose what is required to accomplish that end. Even in the swampy places or in the lows of the journey, a clear focus of the end serves as a catalyst toward endurance. A person with vision is saying, "This is how I plan to live my life, and this is where I am going." A church or an organization with vision is saying, "This is what God has told us to be, and this is what we will be about." We are going to run on and see what the end is going to be, believing all the time that it will be what God has promised.

When we, as set gifts, attain a vision for a group of people, we must understand that what we are seeing is going to sometimes differ dramatically from what the people are seeing. Our challenge, then, is to get people to see as we see, or rather, to see as God sees. In other words, a point of trust and identity must be established if we are to bring our visions to their desired ends. People must be given a span of time wherein they can reach the point of feeling comfortable with or trusting the vision that has been planted into the heart of the set gift. Once trust has been established and people are able to see differently, then we might expect them to do differently.

This leads us to our next chapter, which will encourage us to believe that the vision is to be done and accomplished now. We must remember, however, that just as we have wrestled with God in embracing the vision, we, too, must offer grace to our people. Some of them we will have to wrestle down to get them to see what we see in the realm of the Spirit. Let us, as leaders, learn to master the art of communicating vision in a way that will allow our followers to digest and produce the vision that is in our hearts.

——Chapter 4——
Dealing With Proverbial Syndromes
The Vision Is Now!

May I share with you a word of the Lord that the Holy Spirit revealed to me as I embarked upon another year of leadership in my local assembly? One morning during my *early morning prayer hour*, I heard the voice of the Spirit say emphatically to me, "The Vision Is Now." I remember being grabbed and somewhat startled by this voice and the power of what I heard being told to me. The voice repeated itself as if it was addressing my look of bewilderment and said, "Tell my people, the vision is now." Immediately I began to inquire of the Lord about the bigger picture of this message. Almost simultaneously to my inquiry of the Spirit, I was led to the Book of Ezekiel; and, to my amazement, it contained the very words that the Spirit had spoken unto me. Ezekiel 12:21-28 reads:

> And the word of the LORD came unto me, saying, Son of man, what *is* that proverb *that* ye have in the land of Israel, saying, The days are prolonged, and every vision faileth? Tell them therefore, Thus saith the Lord GOD; I will make this proverb to cease, and they shall no more use it as a proverb in Israel; but say unto them, The days are at hand, and the effect of every vision. For there shall be no more any vain vision nor flattering divination within the house of Israel. For I *am* the LORD: I will speak, and the word that I shall speak shall come to pass; it shall be no more prolonged: for in your days, O rebellious house, will I say

the word, and will perform it, saith the Lord GOD. Again the word of the LORD came to me, saying, Son of man behold, *they of* the house of Israel say, The vision that he seeth *is* for many days *to come*, and he prophesieth of the times *that are* far off. Therefore say unto them, Thus saith the Lord GOD; There shall none of my words be prolonged any more, but the word which I have spoken shall be done, saith the Lord GOD. (*Emphasis added*)

I love the power of this text because it addresses some of the realities around organizational functioning and church longevity. It captures seasons in the life of the vision of organizations when the momentum seems to have ebbed. Therefore, the voice of this text serves as a point of identification for many pastors and leaders who quietly have resigned themselves to the ambiance of defeat. It is a word of the Lord to many who continue to function while hearing the voices of the congregation and observing the behaviors of the masses as they grumble in the pews regarding their disbelief that the organization will make a substantial difference anymore. It flows into the cracks and crevices of the minds of the people who silently believe that the "real days of vision and accomplishments" are over. It sits like a born again believer beside those aged saints who have been so wounded by time that they cannot see life again. And yet the new believer, who has no knowledge of pain or long-term frustrations, sits with excitement, anxiously awaiting the next move of God. So let us hear this text, and may its power speak to those of us in leadership who are in need of a dose of spiritual energy.

Ezekiel is the prophet of the exile. He was deported to

Babylon in the first or second deportation. In his own words, "he sat where the people sat" at the banks of the river of captivity and pondered their ability to survive in a foreign land. He listened to the voices of the people as they sank into hopelessness and as their faith no longer embraced a view of victory and freedom. He watched the people slowly and gradually succumb to the environment of the Babylonians and let go of a unified submission to any leadership that would have given them the capacity to retain positive energy as they endured the countless days of oppression. But most of all, he realized that the vision of the people had been reduced to a zero level and that they had absolutely no view of divine intervention. Consequently, they altered their behaviors to accommodate their faith, which, in my estimation, is a natural response to negative synergism and a dying vision.

The Almighty God visits Ezekiel and gives him a message to declare to the people. Firstly, the word of the Lord is in the form of a question. God asks, "What is this proverb you have in the land of Israel: The days go by and every vision comes to nothing?" God reveals to Ezekiel that He has been listening to the rumblings of the people, that He has inclined His ear to their whispering and their gossip, and that He has been filled to the limit with their excessive and negative talking. When God asks a question, it is totally rhetorical and mainly for the benefit of the ones being questioned. Since God is omniscient and does not lack in any knowledge of human functioning, His method of questioning us is to stir our thinking and help loose us from the grip of that which holds our faith hostage and minimizes our desire to fulfill the macro vision.

Secondly, the Lord emphatically declares to the prophet to

tell the people, "I am going to put an end to the proverb, and they will no longer quote it." This action of the Lord in and of itself is extremely powerful. It suggests that God was about to institute some decisive action, which would reverse the conditions of the Israelites and cause them to see again the goodness of God and to experience restoration and revival. I believe that as we move towards our next challenge of mobilizing people to produce the vision of the Lord, we will see the Divine Manifestation of God in a way that will bring an end to the disenchantment in the hearts of the people. I sense that we are on the horizon of a tremendous move of the Spirit that will stir the people to want to accomplish the vision of the church. Therefore, as leaders, we must be sensitive enough to the Spirit to hear the voice of the Lord saying to us that the days of lack and slack are over, and we must seek instructions on how to shift the people upward towards the vision.

Thirdly, God tells Ezekiel to say to the people, "The days are near when every vision will be fulfilled; none of my words will be delayed any longer; whatever I say will be fulfilled." This third instruction of the Lord focuses on the issue of timing. In spite of the surroundings of the captivity, in spite of the oppression already in motion, God foresaw that the end of the captivity was near and that the beginning of restoration, restitution, and revival was at hand. Every vision that He had revealed to Israel would now come to fruition. The challenge of the people was to discern the timing of the Lord and then allow themselves to be moved by God's voice and timing versus their own pain and disillusioned perspectives.

The heart of this writing is to loudly resound to the hearts of those leaders, whether secular or spiritual, who have become so stagnated by the dynamic of their own pain, coupled with the negative energy and lack of response from the people, that the time is now to accomplish the vision. As a matter of fact, the Holy Spirit gave me a slogan to use for our ministry work as he rejuvenated me to believe again that the vision could be accomplished. The slogan is *"THE VISION IS NOW."* Then God asked me a series of questions:

- **IF NOT NOW, WHEN?**

- **IF NOT NOW, WHY?**

- **IF NOT NOW, WHAT?**

- **IF NOT NOW, HOW?**

As leaders, if we do not accomplish our vision now, then when do we anticipate doing so? If we say that we cannot accomplish it now, but have intentions of doing so in the future, then we must seriously ask ourselves, Why not now? What is it that the future holds that will be more conducive to producing the vision than this present moment? We must determine if we are being guided by our personal pain or by our disappointment with the gap between what we want and where the people seem to be functioning. The question of why not now must be carefully scrutinized and challenged so that we can ascertain whether or not we are victims of the proverbial syndrome in Ezekiel.

We must also ask ourselves, If we are not going to accomplish the vision now, then what are we going to do in the interim? The what-question is important because in it we find the scope of our daily operation and we discover the relevance of what we are doing as it relates to the purpose of our church or organization. The what-question challenges us to discern if we are wasting time or if we are maintaining rituals in our effort to survive with a micro vision mentality. The last question is the "how" issue. How do we continue to motivate people to ascend into a higher realm of functioning and becoming if we as leaders struggle with our own personal motivation towards the same? How do we make it another year leading people in a dismal direction and not having a sense of collective power to get the job done?

All of these questions and the probing of the Scriptures through Ezekiel left me feeling overwhelmed yet motivated to get on with finding a way to accomplish the vision and to effect leadership in the church. It was during these moments of celebrating the positive energy I felt coming from the Holy Spirit that I began to hear Him further. He revealed to me that one of the first challenges of a leader regaining his/her momentum and vision is to get in touch with a fresh revelation of the heart of God. Thus, the Holy Spirit showed me God's heart through the writings of Paul the Apostle in the Book of Ephesians. In Ephesians 1 Paul reveals to the church at Ephesus the mystery of the Gospel. Paul has received a revelation of what God had in His heart before the creation of the world. He tells the church that God chose us (the church) in Him before He created anything. He also reveals that God predestined us to be adopted as Sons through Jesus Christ. Therefore, the church of God must rise up and take dominion in the earth realm and bring about the manifestation of the purpose of God.

In order to accomplish this in the earth realm, God had to release the vision out of His heart and transfer it into the hearts of godly men and women. According to the prophet Jeremiah, God promised to give His people shepherds after His own heart. I am convinced that this means He will give pastors and leaders a glimpse of what He has already accomplished in eternity and will empower them to bring it forth in the earth realm. Therefore, we must get to know His heart and produce it. We cannot allow our pain and people problems to block this revelation in our hearts and spirits. We must hear God and see the vision afresh. After we have the vision burning in our own spirits, then we must convey it to the people until it gets in their hearts. We must identify those who will push to know the heart of the leader as revealed by God.

As I was reflecting over this in prayer, the Holy Spirit graphically illustrated this to me as shown.

THE TIME IS NOW

God's Heart   (Ephesians 1:3-10, 22)

The Pastor's Heart   (Jeremiah 3:15)

The People's Heart (Herein is the challenge: How to get the vision from the Pastor's heart to the heart of the people.)

The more I reflected on what God was saying to me through this passage of Scripture, the more I began to see a deeper issue emerge from its reading. Not only is the struggle in this text a reflection on vision, it also is about leadership. There is a deep cry in this text for the leader to emerge with a sense of direction and hope. There is a longing for a leader to stand firm and relay to the people a word of the Lord that will shift them beyond their despair. There is a calling for a leader to show the people the way and then to create an environment that is conducive towards accomplishing the heart of God. In this text, I repeat, at the risk of redundancy, ***there is a cry for leadership.*** Can we emerge as effective leaders in our congregations and operate in a manner that will bring the church to the fullness of its purpose?

In the next chapter, we will respond to this cry for leadership and examine ways in which we can better prepare ourselves, as leaders, and the people who follow us, to produce the work of God. May I impose a series of questions for us to consider as we move to the next chapter? As we respond to the cry for leadership, we must determine where to begin our exploration of the subject. Do we start with theoretical concepts and constructs on leadership, or do we start with observations about how we are currently practicing leadership? Whose leadership are we inquiring about? These questions and others are helpful in shaping the thinking necessary to embark on the next part of this journey concerning leadership.

———Chapter 5———
A Cry for Leadership: Answering the Call
Examining the Issue of Leadership

As strange as it might seem and as contradictory as it is, the truth is that many churches do not talk about the issue of leadership. We do leadership, but we offer no consistent understanding of the concept of leadership and leaders. We offer no formal training to those we put forth as leaders. We simply say to our people: "God has chosen you and anointed you; I, as Set Gift, have sanctioned you, so now go and do leadership. Exercise your leadership over the elders, or the choir, or the ushers or over one aspect of our congregation." In my estimation, this is a dangerous thing, but we continue to perpetuate it because we are perpetuating our own upbringing in the church—we are creatures of habit. Sometimes, we are so busy that it is easier to just thrust poor old souls out to the vultures and ask them to lead those who are destined to kill, to a place where they give life. What a challenge we impose on the ones we choose to lead, and then we have the audacity to demand good results.

Could it be that as the set gift of the house and as the designated leader in our organizations or groups, we have not focused much on the issue of leadership, and thus, we do not feel astute or equipped enough to teach it to others? Or do we make the erroneous assumption that leadership is something to be done and not taught? Or do we even further assume that people will learn to follow by observing and mimicking what we do as leaders and how we do leadership?

I am not sure as to the reasons we carelessly allow this subject matter to sink into oblivion, but I do know that there is a clarion call for the church to rise to another level in its understanding of leadership. It is critical that the soldiers doing battle are trained for war, and therefore, they must do more than observe the sergeant or the commander. They must be taught the way. It is imperative that football players do more than watch the quarterback, they must get on the field and tackle and run. Why do we, the church with potency and power, let our leaders fall short of the participatory process of leadership development and of the process of gaining knowledge about what it really means to lead?

A good place to start as we seek to develop some uniformity in our thinking about leadership, especially as it relates to the church, is to try to grasp some understanding of what people already know and assume about leadership. As an adult educator, I have always operated under the assumption that when we deal with adult leaders, we must acknowledge what they bring from their own experiences into the context of the environment. Most of the people we work with in our organizations have had previous leadership experiences on some level. Some of the opportunities may have been formal, such as leading in a defined role through the job, work or other church structure; while other opportunities may have been informal, such as leading at home or in a grassroots position in the community. At any rate, we must make a genuine effort to recognize and appreciate the view of leadership that people enter our environment with.

Most of us will lead or follow as we have been subconsciously shaped to do so in our earlier experiences. If we do not lead in the same way, there is a level in which we subconsciously lead—a manner that is somewhat reactive to the context in which we saw leadership modeled. For example, I remember the church in which I first experienced leadership that I am most reactionary to. There were some really wonderful characteristics about my leader that I celebrated way beyond the years of his tenure. I found myself wanting to duplicate these qualities in my own experience of leading people. Yet, almost in a dichotomous manner, I found myself quite resistant to aspects of his leadership that I worked vehemently not to foster in my own organization. As I constantly found myself dancing with the angels and battling with the ghosts from the past leadership experiences, it became increasingly clear to me that part of the struggle that we deal with in leading people can be rooted in our unintentional discounting of their own past and potential. So it is my intention, in the initial phase of this conversation around leadership, to be inclusive of those voices that I have encountered in my own organization, as well as voices of those who have allowed me to conduct workshops and teach classes to them on leadership.

If we understand the root word of the term "education," we would discover that it comes from the Latin word "ducere." This word means "to lead out from." Therefore, the art of educating people has to start at the point from which people come into the context of the learning environment. Herein lies the substantial difference between educating adults and educating children. Adults bring more into the context via their own experiences. This is not to assume that children are empty containers awaiting a mere pouring of water into by the great teacher. Rather, it defines the way in which we begin teaching, or in our case, leading people to some future or some designated place of being or doing or becoming.

When we as leaders engage in the task of leading those around us, we must allow ourselves to take in what people bring into the context. Sometimes, it is like taking in a breath of fresh air; while at other times, it is like sniffing at the odorous intake of polluted air. Once we take in that air, it becomes part of the natural makeup of who we are, and then we seek to shape and define our lives.

In light of the above suggestions, let me share with you some of the views I have gotten over the span of my teaching, regarding the subject of leadership. One of my favorite questions to ask, after engaging people in a fictitious scenario such as the Keep-A-Gap Church, is "How do you define leadership?" As simple as the question is, it always gives me valuable insight as to how to engage the group in any further exercise of studying leadership. My favorite set of responses originated when I did a workshop for the Greater Mt. Calvary Holy Church in Washington, DC, where the honorable Bishop Alfred and Susie Owens are pastors. I was conducting a workshop with a group of approximately fifty of their ministers. When I posed this question, it immediately became clear to me that I was dealing with a very sophisticated and educated group, many of whom had grappled and struggled very seriously with this notion of leadership. Some of the group's responses are listed below.

- *Leadership is possessing the quality to lead, which entails having the ability to plan, to set goals, to share vision and to motivate people.*

- *Leadership is focused guidance towards a pre determined goal.*

- *Leadership is seeing a need, and then having a desire to do, and aiming within your authority, capacity and ability to meet the need.*

- *Leadership is the ability to structure, influence and guide people to reach a desired goal.*

- *Leadership is being first partaker of what you are instructing others to do.*

- *Leadership is the ability to pour into people.*

- *Leadership is the reconciliation of intellect, moral character, and comprehensive powers that allow control, as well as inspiration.*

- *Leadership is taking directions from the Holy Spirit and organizing people.*

In a class that I taught on leadership in the Down East Christian Leadership Training Institute, I also was given some definitions that I enjoyed listening to as the students expounded upon them further. Some of them are:

- *Leadership is the ability to inspire others to become and fulfill themselves by example.*

- *Leadership is the ability to establish a certain order or way, and then to cause others to move according to that way.*

- *Leadership is motivating others to work together with a common purpose.*

There is one final piece that I would like to share as we

move towards a definition of leadership. In one of the Institute classes, we defined leadership as *an invitation, from a designated person, for those following, to come and go with that person on a journey towards accomplishing a particular purpose or goal.* The origin of this definition stems from our understanding of how Jesus, as a designated leader, invited his disciples to come and go with him. According to Mark 1:18-20, when Jesus identified those whom he wanted to be a part of his leadership team, he issued them an invitation:

> *Now as he walked by the sea of Galilee, he saw Simon and Andrew his brother casting a net into the sea: for they were fishers. And Jesus said unto them, Come ye after me, and I will make you to become fishers of men. And straightway they forsook their nets, and followed him. And when he had gone a little farther thence, he saw James the son of Zebedee, and John his brother, who also were in the ship mending their nets. And straightway he called them: and they left their father Zebedee in the ship with the hired servants, and went after him.* (*Emphasis added*)

So I asked the class if this is what we wanted to lift up on this particular morning as a working definition for leadership; then what would they need to accept my invitation, as a designated leader, to come and go with me. I almost feel a need to offer a disclaimer around my own acceptance of this definition because it is clear to me that it lacks a large part of what leadership is about. This definition reminds me of the "Great Man" theory as an appropriate model for leadership. While I do think that such theory is extremely applicable in the case of Jesus, and while I recognize that it has certainly had its place in our historical movement of how leadership has been defined, I do not, however, espouse it as an appropriate model for these current times. For the purposes of inclusiveness and diversity, I thought it important to share this conversation. The responses around what they needed as followers were:

1. *For the leader to know the vision.*

2. *Traveling tools, i.e., understanding, direction, guidance.*

3. *Faith in the leader.*

4. *Methods or steps to show us how to follow.*

5. *Need to know the big picture and how individual purposes fit in.*

6. *Need to see what the leader sees.*

7. *To be shown the benefits of the experience being for all and not just the leader.*

8. *To know that the leader can drive.*

9. *Trust in the leader (this may be earned or bestowed).*

10. *To know how I, as a follower, can help bring clarity around my own role.*

What became clear to us in this exercise is that leadership involves helping people move from a place of origin to a place where there is some mutual end goal that the group desires to attain. If people are to follow the leader, then they need clarity with each step they take. As a result of this understanding, the class proposed the following diagram as a graphic image of the steps required to take the journey with the leader in a manner in which they felt fulfilled and inspired.

The class used the steps to show that on the very first level the follower needs knowledge in order to go with the leader. People who follow leadership have a very basic need to know the vision of the leader. They desire to hear his/her heart and to hear the leader declare the vision on a constant basis. Secondly, the class saw equipping as a necessary step. This step is basically about empowerment. The class felt that when followers have a sense of being empowered, it is easier for them to participate in producing the vision because the leaders have invested in them through training and development. Thirdly, the class lifted up the concept of faith. In a very simple way, they proposed that followers just want to know and believe that the vision given to them by the leader came from God. This will lead to the fourth step of trust. Trust involves respecting the leader and believing that he/she has been with God enough to conceive the vision. Finally, the class said that they needed to know the benefits. They want to know how their participation in the vision will work for them in a reciprocal manner.

As we move now toward a working definition for this book, I must say that I am not writing this book for the purpose of creating a new definition of leadership, nor am I trying to conjure up some unique twist on the issue of leadership. However, after engaging in the process of studying leadership over the years, I have finally come upon a definition that I think most accurately captures my heartbeat. This is a definition that I discovered through my work with the Wildacres Leadership Program of North Carolina. One of the primary texts this group uses to study leadership is the book *Leadership Without Easy Answers*, by Ronald Heifetz. Heifetz is the director of the Leadership Education Project at the John F. Kennedy School of Government at Harvard University.

Heifetz looks at leadership as more of an activity rather than a position of authority in a social structure or as a personal set of characteristics. He proposes that leadership should be examined in what he terms "adaptive work." Thus, leadership is concerned with the learning required to address conflicts in the values people hold. Leadership is about understanding what is necessary to diminish the gap between the values people stand for and the reality they face.

Out of my fascination with Heifetz's work, the sub-title of this book was born: *Understanding How to Bridge the Gap Between the Leader and the People.* I struggled with many iterations of this title as I attempted to integrate the work of Heifetz with my own struggle around wanting the issue of leadership to be studied more in the church environment. As I stated at the outset of this chapter, leadership is something that the church does, but not necessarily something that it studies consistently. In pondering how to get the subject on the table, I remembered that my own personal struggle with leading people was probably more common than I knew. After conversing with several other pastors and leaders around this issue, and especially after presenting the workshop at Greater Mt. Calvary, I knew then that I needed to use this book as a tool to help us as a church develop a platform from which to talk about leadership.

Therefore, my first notions around the book title were "Helping the Set Gift Bridge the Gap." The intent here was to focus on ways in which this book could tap into the adaptive work necessary to diminish the gap between what the visionary sees and the level of productivity seen in the people who have to carry out the vision of the leader. While this statement may sound scary to those reading this book, the truth of the matter is that for most of us as church leaders (and the manner in which we have historically interpreted our calling), the role of the people is to follow the vision of the leader. I am not knocking nor belittling this way of how the church has defined its leadership. I am proposing, however, that within this assumption around our view of leadership, we create pitfalls that arise because of a limited view of the vision and because of a deficit in knowing what work is necessary to make the vision a collective and synergistic one. When there is collective vision, there exists a synergy which allows the organization, church or group to accomplish more of its desired end. This comes as a result of the cooperative way in which people work together.

In order to create this synergistic functioning, we must find a way to diminish the gap between what we envision as leaders and what the people envision as followers. Heifetz's definition would suggest that this requires some form of adaptive work. As we examine the work of Jesus' ministry, we see that the closer the followers were to knowing and understanding the vision in His heart, the more productive they were in carrying out the work. The closer they were to His heart, the less there was a gap between what he was called to execute by His Father and what the disciples actually did in helping him produce that work. The following diagram illustrates my thinking around this issue.

In terms of Jesus' operation, the closer the disciples were to his heart, the more productive they were in terms of producing what was in his heart.

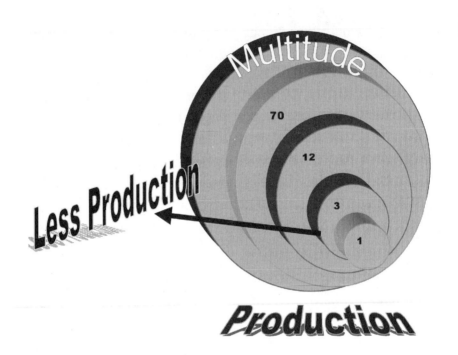

In the above diagram, 1 = John; 3 = Peter, James, John; 12 = the disciples; 70 = those sent out 2 by 2; and the multitude = the masses who followed Jesus from place to place.

According to this diagram, Jesus ministered to the multitude and taught them the way of the word. This group was the least willing to submit to the teachings and the ways of Jesus because they were more enamored with his doings and his working of miracles than with understanding what he was trying to accomplish from a visionary perspective. Next, Jesus had the 70 whom he was able to send out in two's. But even they came back with a report of being excited over the miracle syndrome and the fact that demons responded to the authority of Jesus. Evidently, they did not know his heartbeat and that the real issue was not the miracles but the manifestation of God's love through Jesus. As we move beyond the 70, we see Jesus' greater level of influence and change in terms of creating an environment that would be conducive to the productivity that occurred when he dealt with the twelve, the three, and the one.

It is interesting to note that it was the three—Peter, James and John—whom Jesus invited into the Garden of Gethesemane to share his most painful experience and most difficult challenge as a leader. The less we feel the gap between those we know share our hearts in our vision and what we have in our hearts as leaders, the more likely we are to let the three see our sweat, our blood and our tears. Every leader, while in the process of doing leadership, needs someone intimate enough with him/her, and therefore able to see us in the heat of our struggles. We all need someone we can trust to take a handkerchief and wipe our sweat, to put a tourniquet around us to stop the bleeding, and to take a towel and dry our tears. We need those whom we can be naked before and yet not get trapped by our nakedness. These are the ones we groom and mentor for the leadership mantel.

It is equally as fascinating to discover that as John laid his head on Jesus' bosom at the Last Supper, there was an exchange of something between the two of them that drew John even closer to the heart of Jesus. The imagery and symbolism of this disciple at the table with Jesus, pressed against His heart, is a powerful image of what I think should be conveyed about leadership. We must find a way to empower those around us to the degree that they are not afraid of or inhibited from putting their heads on our spiritual chests (or our leadership bosom) and hear the throbbing of our hearts as we execute the tasks assigned to us.

As we run this race of leadership, fight the good fight with all the challenges we must encounter, and as we become determined to finish our course, we must be sure that we are sharing our visions and closing the gap between those who follow us, and ourselves. We must identify the one to whom we would entrust our most prized possession or our most precious treasures of our vision. To the one disciple on Jesus' bosom, he entrusted his mother. What an awesome image of us as leaders, entrusting that which has been with us for years, that which we gave birth to, and that which we have poured our lives out for, to the one we endear as being able to take care of it after we have gone.

While we may not be able to get all of our congregants or even all of those who share with us in the leadership process to be unified and at a state where the vision is empowered, we must try to glean from the previous model regarding Jesus' leadership. The production level of these groups, in terms of their ability to produce what was in the heart of Jesus, increased and was more effective because they "shared in the vision" with Jesus. This is attributable to the fact that they got to know His heart and he simultaneously had an opportunity to know their hearts and abilities.

What impresses me greatly about Jesus was his ability to

create a way in which we could be as close to him as any of those who walked with him. The Apostle Paul, one of the greatest revelators of the mysteries of God, demonstrates this in a most powerful way in the Book of Philippians. Paul declares, "I want to know him." I want to know him in Resurrection, to know Him in Suffering, and to know Him in Death. Paul knew that only when he knew Jesus intimately could he then most effectively reveal Him. So he pursued God through the Spirit and thus captured the mysteries of the heart of God concerning the church.

We, as leaders, must encourage those who follow us to get to know our hearts and our spirits. We must encourage them to pursue us through pursuing God. I am convinced that there is a correlation between those who pursue our hearts and those who pursue Christ and see us out of a residual of having seen Christ. I believe that as worship occurs, flowing from the throne room of heaven will be insights on how to produce the heart of God in the set gift.

Using this understanding, I would like to rehearse our proposed definition of leadership, and then use the scenario of the Keep-A-Gap Pentecostal Church as a tool to explore ways to identify what must be done to create a synergistic organization model of leadership. In the next two diagrams, I will lift up what I first see as my interpretation of Heifetz's model of leadership, and then I will lift up my own model of leadership as it connects to the vision in the heart of the set gift. Heifetz proposes the following:

LEADERSHIP

Reality ➡ What We Value

> **Leadership is about mobilizing people to do the**
> *adaptive work of merging our realities with what*
> *we value.*

Let us choose one of the issues in the scenario of the Keep-A-Gap Church to apply this model. If we look at the list generated at the beginning of the book, one clearly identified issue is that of "Tithing." It seems that the value of the pastors in the church was based on their biblical understanding that tithing is important to the church and that all should be paying 10 percent of their earnings to the church. While this seemed to have been stated as being important to the church, the records indicate that only about 47 percent of the people were actually tithing. Therefore, 53 percent of the people either have not caught the vision of the leaders or there is some hidden factor within this church as to why the people are tithing at such a low percentage. Our model of leadership would suggest that there is "adaptive work" which must be done within this church if it is going to achieve its goal of maximum tithing.

When I think of the starting place for the adaptive work, I first start with values. The question that I raise around trouble-shooting this tithing issue is, "Whose value is it that we pay tithes?" Is it possible that the pastors in this church are operating off of the assumption that all those in attendance value the concept of paying tithes? Perhaps some work needs to be done around adopting the tithing principle as a shared value of the congregation and not just as a "pastoral value." The question becomes, What must be done in order to get the issue to become a shared value of the community?

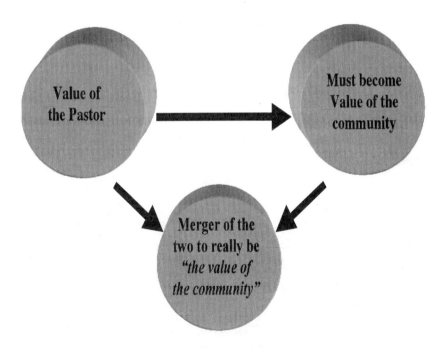

In other words, the value of the pastor must actually become the "value of the community." When it becomes the value of the community, there is no gap between pastor and community. Rather, they are both mutually inclusive. The language then changes from "the pastor wants us to pay tithes" to, rather, "the community believes in and values tithing" as a biblical principle and as a way of operating.

This view is consistent, however, with what we just proposed regarding the power of the Spirit to convey the heart of the pastor by first revealing the heart of God. As individuals walk in communion with God, they will come to know that God wants them to pay tithes, and not just the pastors. They will ascend to know quickly that the pastors are only acting consistently with the Scriptures. Thus, it is easier to reach a communal value regarding tithing rather than just interpreting tithing as a pastoral mandate.

My own proposal of a model for leadership is an adaptation of Heifetz' model. The difference in the two is rooted in my own need to connect vision to the level of functioning, as well as a need to use a language that is more relevant to church organizations. For me, leadership is about identifying an appropriate "Intervention Process" which will determine what must be done in the interim between what the visionary initially envisions and the actual desired outcome. In my proposal, the visionary sees the "telois" of the vision at the outset. This word "telois" is a Greek term implying "perfect, the end as it should be." He/she must then engage in the process of determining what is necessary to produce the vision in a way which is commensurate with what is in the visionary's heart. I am calling this state of the heart the "end of the vision," which the visionary sees at the outset.

The following diagram illustrates my view as to how clear vision imparted by God, in the beginning, becomes a type of map to keep us intact with the movement of our ministry and work from beginning to end.

The Process of Intervention

The Beginning of Vision = A Revelation of the End of the Vision Telois

What to do? When to do it? How to do it?

Who does what? Has the vision been written? Has it been made plain?

The End of Vision = The people are doing what we envisioned them doing

The whole notion of leadership is not about one person declaring that they have been given a vision by God, as much as it is the ability of that person, in conjunction with others and/or those following, to accomplish the work necessary in the intervention process to produce the desired outcomes. Sometimes, the work necessary in the interim, or intervention stage, can be extremely simple if there are not a lot of complexities around the issues or if the leadership team shares the same values. At other times, the work in the intervention process can be extremely difficult and painful if the leadership team and the followers have a gulf between them. At any rate, the challenge of leadership is about identifying ways to diminish the gap, regardless of its size, and to help bring the vision to fruition.

I first heard a preacher by the name of Miles Munroe talk about this concept of God showing us the end of a thing and then backing us up to start at the beginning. So many times, the reason that our vision fails or the reason that we do not understand what is necessary to bring leadership along in a proper relation to the vision is that we try to start the vision at its end point. But every vision is first birthed in the spirit domain of man or conceived in the mind. In the outset of this birthing of the vision, we get a glimpse of the vision in its fruition, or state of maturity.

It is similar to a woman giving birth to a child. I can imagine at the moment that the child enters the world, the woman is filled with dreams of the accomplishments of this child and sees the child operating in his/her fullness at a given point in life. Sometimes she sees that the child has graduated from an Ivy League school and has landed a job on Wall Street and is bringing home a six-figure income. She also sees that the child has found a spouse and all of the grandchildren are over at her house on the holidays; the fireplace is burning and everyone is laughing and overjoyed. She sees herself sitting in the corner of the family room overwhelmed with tears as she experiences the bliss of this moment. Then, all of a sudden, the baby cries in her arms and the momentary fantasy is over. She must snap out of her dream and back up to the beginning and start with comforting the baby's cry—inviting her husband to join in the celebration of this moment—and then make preparation to take the child home.

This woman had to do what every visionary must encounter

as they try to engage people in the leadership process. Once they have conceived the vision in the spirit, they must now "let the vision be born twice." The second birthing of this vision is giving birth to it in the natural. Just as this woman had to exit her dream world and give birth to a natural process of caring for this child, so must we as leaders do the same. We must back up to the beginning and allow the vision to be born in the natural. This second birthing is what I am terming as "the intervention process." The question that must be answered at this point of the journey is, What work is necessary to bring into the realm of the natural, that which we conceived and saw in the realm of the spiritual? Heifetz would probably ask, "What adaptive work is necessary to reach the desired goal?"

It is in the next chapter of this book that I would like to explore with you the work necessary to close the gap between what we envision as the end point and the realities that we encounter along the way. As we move towards this, let me state, up front, a few assumptions I bring into the context of doing leadership work. First of all, I operate out of the assumption that the work is ever-evolving. Due to the fact that a lot of work in the intervention stage is mostly progressive and evolutionary in nature, it requires that we celebrate the fact that the closer we get to our goals, the more work sometimes is required.

Secondly, I operate out of the assumption that the work necessary to produce the vision will be both proactive and reactive. Every leader must, in conjunction with the team players, develop proactive strategies for accomplishing organizational vision. There must be an action plan. In spite of all of our best efforts, there will arise the need to develop reactive strategies due to our humanity and to the demands of the evolution process. When one deals with living organisms, such as those we work and operate in, there are constant changes which are cumulative in nature. Thus, some things become unpredictable and uncontrollable until after they have occurred at least once. Therefore, we know that even at our best, there will always be failure, regrouping and adjusting in trying to get people to produce the vision of the organization.

Thirdly, I operate out of the assumption that as leaders, we must be free and unafraid to let the work and the process help define the next steps. Fear that adjustments and adaptations are negative elements will cause us to insert interventions and control mechanisms that can be damaging. We must trust God, as the Master of the vision, to guide it to its end. We must also trust ourselves, as laborers together with God, to be able to make healthy decisions regarding the adaptive work.

Let's now turn to look at some of the necessary work in the intervention process that will help us accomplish our goals and desired ends.

—Chapter 6—
Bridging the Gap

Let's now return to the scenario of the Keep-A-Gap Pentecostal Church and see if we can identify the adaptive work necessary in the intervention stage that will allow this church to function at its maximum capacity. As we do this, I encourage you to join in the process by releasing your mind to engage in how you, as a leader or follower, would endeavor to help this church diminish the gap in its experience of leadership. Let's further assume that we have been called in as consultants to help get this church to diminish the gap between the desired goals of the leaders and the current mode of functioning of the people. In our consultation, we will try to identify what must occur in the intervention stages that will enable the leaders of this church to produce the vision that God has given them. We will further try to create proposed solutions to some of the identified issues that this church continues to struggle with.

I asked the group at Greater Mount Calvary to help me identify the issues of leadership as it related to this church. Listed below are some of the areas they identified:

- *A lack of teaching*

- *Lack of leader's ability*

- *Continuing identity with accountability and responsibility (Each area has to revisit its own accountability and responsibility towards this problem)*

- *Goals have not been revisited*

- *Lack of communication from the pastor*

- *Core group not being reached; some deficit in operation*

When we look at the issues of the Keep-A-Gap Church, there can be much debate regarding whether or not the issue is a "leadership" problem or a "followership" problem. The manner in which we attempt to solve some of the issues in this church will be contingent upon our view of "whose problem it is." Imagine a continuum, which contains two extremes:

Responsibility for the Dynamics of the Church
Point A   Point B

The Pastors   The Congregation

Point A represents the responsibility for leadership resting solely with the pastors, while Point B represents the sole responsibility of the problem lying with the followers. This kind of divergent thinking only exacerbates the problem. It will result in pitching the pastors and the followers against each other versus creating a dynamic for joint ownership of the problems, leading to shared solutions.

If we assume that the problems rest solely with the pastors of the church, then all of our energy will be invested in trying to change or fix them so that they will be better able to lead the congregation. If we operate out of the assumption that the real problem lies with the followers, then we will concentrate on ways to fix the people. I call this "either/or" thinking.

In "either/or" thinking, we create a dichotomy that ultimately pitches the pastors against the people, or vice versa. This is not good because it creates competition and sometimes breeds animosity between two groups that are actually on the same team. War breaks out between the pastors and the leaders, and then we spiritualize this dynamic by calling it "spiritual warfare." While this is true, it is spiritual warfare that is unnecessary. The truth of the matter is I am not sure we can "fix" people anyway. Fixing people is a job for Jesus.

You and I both have witnessed congregations that have taken on a critical spirit in regard to their leaders. Once this happens, the leaders are seen through a looking glass and everything they do becomes annoying to people. We also have witnessed congregations that are under attack by the leadership. Rather than properly troubleshooting the negative dynamics in the congregation, the leaders have resorted to a series of complaints about how negligent the congregation is, how it disregards leadership, and how it fails to grow up and become mature enough to produce the work of the ministry. What is even worse is that sometimes both of the groups are at odds and at war at the same time. As a result, Sunday morning becomes a time to see who has more power and to see who can outlast the attacks coming from both the pulpit and the pew. Poor Jesus gets caught somewhere between the two and probably feels that he is being crucified afresh, so He quickly makes his exodus and goes to a church where he is welcomed and wanted.

I would like to invite us to challenge our paradigm of "either/or" thinking and move to one of "both/and" thinking. The "both/and" paradigm assumes that the existing problems were ultimately created by both the pastors and the leaders, and therefore must be worked on simultaneously by both. It suggests that there is adjustment and adaptive work required on the part of the pastors as well as the people. I will proceed using this paradigm as our model of operation.

Pastors, may I talk about us for a few moments? I recognize that this can be quite challenging because it seems as if we are always blamed for so many things in the church. When people are sick, they blame us for not showing up soon enough. When someone dies, they blame us for not visiting long enough. When someone is hurt, they blame us for saying or doing the wrong thing. Our sermons are too long or too short, or they are too meaty or too milky. Our clothes are too dressy or flashy, or they are too outdated and cheap. We demand too much money and time from the people, and we are insensitive to their needs. And the list could go on and on.

So I know that I am at risk when I embark upon a solution that starts with us as pastors first. I do, however, invite you to "try on" my thinking of "both/and," and let's explore together ways in which we as pastors can do things differently or more succinctly, which will produce a higher level of functioning from our people. Will you give me permission to talk about us? Can we call this section "Straight Talk to Pastors"?

The Holy Spirit impressed upon my spirit that there are some definite things that we must do as leaders to empower ourselves. In many ways, we stand as a liaison between God and the people. We are the conduits for the outpouring of God's word and message to be channeled through. We are spokespersons for the Master. As the Apostle Paul declared, we are ambassadors for Christ. Therefore, it is incumbent upon us to be spiritually postured to receive of the Lord ourselves. We must first "receive" before we can "release."

STRAIGHT TALK TO PASTORS

As we embark on this dimension of the work, I would like to lift up six substantive elements of leadership that I believe are critical to the success of our ministries. I call these substantive elements because they belong to the "nature of leadership." In other words, leadership without them is faulty leadership. These elements are:

1) PRAYER
2) VISION
3) SHARED VISION
4) DESIGN
5) EXECUTION
6) INTERVENTION

The more I interact with these substantive elements in producing the work of the ministry, the more I am convinced that there is some type of cyclical relationship among them.

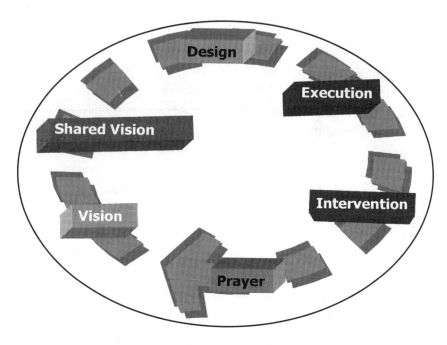

Cyclical Relationship among Substantive Elements

It seems that one element gives birth to the next via the Holy Spirit. I believe that the Holy Spirit hovers over us as we engage in each task. When the moment is ripe or when there is some degree of "readiness" on our behalf, as determined by the Spirit, then the Holy Spirit releases His wind upon us and we are given an invitation to move to the next task.

In a sense, this is a type of "waiting on the Lord." We must master the skill of waiting until He releases us or "blows us into the next task." The challenge for some of us is learning to harness our drives and ambitions in a healthy way that will not prematurely cause us to produce the work of the ministry in our flesh versus in the realm of the Spirit. This can be a sensitive issue, however, particularly when we as leaders see so many around us producing tremendous visions and doing great feats in the kingdom. As we struggle with the culture of success around us, we can get impatient and feel compelled to get out there as quickly as possible.

Those of us who have been on the battlefield a long time and those who have produced mega ministries would probably quickly attest to the fact that timing is critical as it relates to one being able to sustain what is produced. Waiting on the Lord is a type of safeguard for the execution phase. This is true for many reasons. One reason is that there is always security in knowing that you only brought forth what God wanted. Secondly, God will always protect His own. So if He releases you to do, then you can count on Him to take care of what He told you to do. Thirdly, it limits the mental attacks and satanic accusations that can be imposed upon you because you released ownership to the Master. Even in all of this, we as leaders will still have to encounter warfare. If we wait on the Lord, at least we will be at our maximum position to do battle.

As we attempt to gain insight into each of these elements, let me identify the outline by which we are suggesting that we do the work of leadership.

1. PRAYER
   A.   LET EVERYTHING BE BORN TWICE
   B.   ENTER THE HOLY OF HOLIEST

2. VISION
   A.   WRITE THE VISION

    B.   MAKE IT PLAIN

3. SHARED VISION
    A.   COMMUNICATION
    B.   ASKING THE APPROPRIATE QUES-
           TIONS
    C.   KNOWING WHO YOUR FRIENDS
           ARE

4. DESIGN
    A.   CREATION
    B.   STRATEGIES
          1. INFRASTRUCTURE
          2. TRAINING DEVELOPMENT

5. EXECUTION—RELEASING PEOPLE

6. INTERVENTION—SEE CHAPTER FIVE

Step One: *DISCOVERING THE POWER OF PRAYER*

I was blessed in my life to have a mother whose life was filled with intercessory prayer. She lived, breathed and ate prayer on a daily basis, and this is no exaggeration. She taught me the power of prayer and the results of prayer. Sadly to say, my life was so busy when I first started to pastor, that my personal prayer life was squeezed in between ripping and running and doing ministry for my Lord. In spite of my own "minimum prayer life," God honored the prayers of my mother. She would pray for the church, for the pastor, for the members, and for all the issues that would arise in the church. It was after she went home to be with the Lord that I experienced the power of her prayer mantle being transferred to my life. It seemed as if all that she taught me about prayer and all that she stood for came to pass in my life as she ascended to glory.

I remember God speaking to me one morning as I was wrestling with some problems in the church, and He reminded me of one of the lessons my mother had taught regarding prayer. Her statement to me was, "If it can't be birthed in prayer and bathed in prayer, then it does not need to be in the church." God challenged me about some of the programs we had in the church, some of the leaders that I chosen and, more poignantly, some of the things that I had declared to be the will of the Lord for the church. It was in prayer that God told me, *"Let everything be born twice."*

The Spirit of the Lord reminded me of how some things got accomplished in the church, in the past. There is a way in which my mother had birthed things in prayer before the Holy Spirit had given me instructions as to how to bring them forth in the natural. Now that she was gone, I had to learn to lay before God myself and allow Him to birth in my spirit through prayer, what He wanted to be birthed in the natural in the church. In other words, the vision of God had to be birthed in the spiritual dimension first. Then I had to learn to bathe it in prayer on a daily basis and let it simmer in the prayer pot for a few days before I decided to serve the vision to the people. Only after I had gotten a release in prayer should I allow it to be born in the natural with the people.

What I am suggesting to us as pastors and leaders, is that we should not underestimate the power of prayer as we bring forth the vision of the Lord. Part of the resistance that people give us can be counteracted by our own unquestionable confidence that what we are asking of them has been refined in the furnace with the Lord.

Sometimes it is difficult to admit that what we put on the table with the people came out of our spiritual quest for doing the right thing, but it was channeled too quickly through our personality and our humanity. As a result, it did not have maximum clarity regarding what was "good and God" versus what was "good and not all God."

If I may regress for a moment, I see a model of the tabernacle of Moses being significant to this issue of bathing our God-given vision in prayer. Remember that Moses was given instructions to create three courts in the tabernacle. The outer court was for all to enter and contained items made of brass. Brass could symbolize "our humanity," and thus could represent our desire as leaders to get the heartbeat of God for ministry. Therefore, we enter the tabernacle at its entrance place as mere flesh and mere man, seeking the revelation of God to be birthed in our hearts. The truth of the matter is that God does speak in the outer court and give to us His revelations. We must be careful at this point not to turn and depart from the tabernacle and quickly declare what God showed us.

We must allow ourselves to press further into the next court. It was in the next court, or in the inner court, that God told Moses to place the golden candelabras, the table of showbread and the altar of incense. These items were made with wood but overlaid with gold. The use of both gold and wood symbolizes God and man in the same court. I am suggesting that when we as leaders feel God birthing a vision in us or giving us directions as to how to lead the church of God, we must take that initial vision and press into the inner court so that God can bring clarity. Usually, it is in this inner place with God that we can feel the Holy Spirit separate our ideas from

His and/or take our thinking into a place of purity. Once this happens, we must be careful not to make a quick exit back to the congregation and release the vision to the people. Our haste to get the vision in the hands of the people and our excitement to bring forth what we have seen can become a barrier to us because we have released the vision before its proper time and have utilized improper methodologies for the vision.

We must do as God told Moses, as He showed him the purpose of the innermost court. As priests of the Most High God, we must push beyond the veil where there is nothing but the Ark of the Covenant and the Mercy Seat. Since these items are made purely of gold, they represent "All God." I believe that this is the place that all pastors and leaders must enter before we release the vision into the hands of the people. We must press into prayer with the vision in our hearts and move into the innermost court and experience nothing but God. It is in this place that I believe God will anoint us to be able to bring the vision back to the people in a way that they will recognize the glory of the Lord upon us. When they see the presence of God upon us, they will be inclined to listen and to hear the revelation. People usually will not fight with God as much as they will struggle with the leaders. However, even after exiting the place of the Presence of God, we must be careful as to how we deliver the vision to the people. I am under the persuasion that if we put the vision in a defined form, it will be easier for us to share; and this, in turn, will create continuity as the vision is shared from one level of leadership to the next.

Step Two: *WRITE THE VISION*

After the vision is birthed and bathed in prayer, one of the first things that the leader should do is to make an attempt to capture the essence of the vision on paper. He/she should write the vision and make it plain. I would suggest to all leaders—regardless as to what level of leadership they are encountering or what type of organization or whether the organization is secular or spiritual—to invest time in writing what they see as the vision for the people. This writing of the vision of the organization will help the leader identify what work is necessary to accomplish the vision. Simultaneously, it will give the leader a roadmap to follow when leading becomes swampy or confusing, or when it seems as if there is a breakdown in the strength of the organization. It will also make it very easy for others to follow the leader and understand how to best engage in the mutual process of bringing the vision to pass.

Such a notion of writing the vision is espoused strongly in the writings of Habakkuk the prophet. Habakkuk tells the people to "write the vision, and make it plain upon tables, that he may run that readeth it" (Habakkuk 2:2). I see two possible interpretations of what Habakkuk is suggesting. First, I see the prophet telling the leader to write the vision so clearly that when the vision enters the hearts of the people, it will be so fresh and so alive and so clearly stated that they will take off running to share the vision with others. This to me feels like a synergistic moment: when the energy in the running of the feet of the people becomes a part of the dynamics and makes the vision become greater than its original isolated state.

The second notion that I see is that Habakkuk is suggesting to the people to write the vision so plainly, as if they were putting it up on a billboard. It would be posted in a way that was so clear that as the people ran from place to place, they could always see the vision from whatever station or place they were in at a given time. I can envision our leaders now, excited about what they understand and running with steam and swiftness to declare this vision to others.

Step Three: *CREATING A SHARED VISION*

The third piece of work, which must occur in the intervention process, is that of finding a way to make the written vision a shared vision of the people. This is a piece of the adaptive work that must not be omitted or minimized. Not only must we write the vision, we must communicate it in a way that is conducive to people being able to understand it, buy into it, and be willing to make the vision a shared one. Shared vision is created when there is obvious synergy in the organization. The pastors have successfully conveyed the vision in a manner that allows the people to hear the vision, see the vision, and to participate in some sense of ownership of the vision. I am convinced that people operate best when they have tapped into the heart of the leader and are able to see themselves as creators and sustainers of the vision on the table.

The leader has to ask the hard question: How do I share the vision and retain its authenticity and purity, while simultaneously allowing the people to share input which will give them a sense of ownership? I call this phenomenon "dancing on the tightrope." Dancing on the tightrope is scary business, especially if we espouse the process of prayer that was proposed at the beginning of this chapter. The pivotal question becomes, How can I take what I have been given by God and what I have carried through three courts of prayer, and then submit it into the hands of a people who will take it and trample it with their own thinking? The tension in the tightrope dance increases as we reflect upon all the hurt and pain we have experienced from yesterdays release of the vision to the people. In spite of this fear, all leaders must learn to dance on the tightrope and not be afraid of what this means. I do believe that there is a way in which we can submit our visions to the people, allow them to grapple with and refine them, and then offer criticisms and suggestions that will not reduce the ultimate intent of the visions.

In my experience, I have discovered that this is best done through the use of a team of mature elders and through those leaders who are closest to the pastor's heart. We can only entrust the first level of exposure of the vision to those who love God and love us as leaders. They are not our flunkies, nor are they just "yes" people. Rather, they are the ones who, over time, have stood with us, have flunked and failed with us, and have come to know us in a more intimate context. They know how to take what we put on the table, and in the same manner as we did, walk through the three courts of prayer and return to us with insights and revelations that will help cause the vision to prosper and come to fruition. May I suggest that it is very dangerous to take that which we have labored intensely over and then give it to those who have not suffered with us and who do not have the best interest of the church in mind. We must learn who our friends are.

My definition of friends is not a buddy-buddy issue. I am speaking of those who have drunk from the same cup as we have and who have served God and us in such a way that they are mature enough to protect the revelation of God over their relationship with others. I am talking about friends in the context which Jesus uses in John 15:14-15: "You are my friends if you do what I command. I no longer call you servants, because a servant does not know his master's business. Instead, I have called you friends, for everything that I learned from my Father I have made known to you." Once we know whom the Lord's friends are—ones that we mutually call our friends—then we can entrust the vision to them and invite their input in a manner that creates shared vision. Remember, if they are not friends of Jesus, then they are certainly not friends of ours, as leaders. The purpose for releasing the vision into this level of leadership is to be able to design a strategy that will help get the vision accomplished.

Step Four: *DESIGNING A PROPER STRATEGY*

As leaders, we must never underestimate the power of a proper design for the work we must create. Major corporations spend millions of dollars on design leaders, design teams—and the designs. The leaders of these organizations have come to know that their profitability is an outcome or residual of design. Therefore, they put their money where their hope is. I believe that we as the church of God must spend more time examining our design and our strategies for producing ministry.

Design is a subsequent step to vision. It cannot and must not precede vision. When we shift the order, we are actually putting the cart before the horse. Yet, you and I know many leaders and pastors who either copy other people's designs, and then try to give vision to their churches, or they just sort of do their thing without design and call it vision. There is a major danger in this type of functioning. I believe that if we properly focus on the first three recommended steps of prayer, writing the vision and sharing it with the appropriate leaders, then design will feel natural and logical.

If you are a new leader or a pastor at the outset of your ministry, then you have the good fortune of creating a design before you run into the pitfalls of the vision being cast into the swamp or hauled into the graveyard of dead visions. I urge you, by the grace of God offered me in retrospect, to take the time to invest in creating the proper design and strategies to produce the vision in your heart. Go back to the intervention model in Chapter 5 and see what steps are necessary.

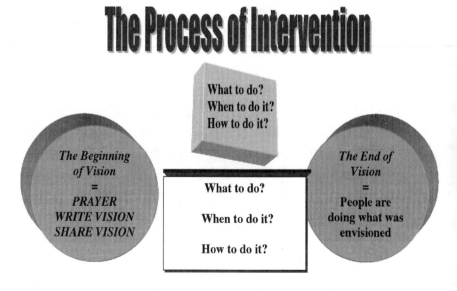

The Process of Intervention

What to do?
When to do it?
How to do it?

The Beginning
of Vision
=
PRAYER
WRITE VISION
SHARE VISION

What to do?

When to do it?

How to do it?

The End of
Vision
=
People are
doing what was
envisioned

The leaders who are beginning this process should spend ample time exploring the questions around what to do, how to do it, when to do it, who should do it, has the vision been written and has it been made plain. This certainly will save a whole lot of headaches and heartaches in the future. Time invested in the creation will certainly be time saved in the execution. For those of us who have been on the battlefield beyond the beginning phase, we must also enter the intervention process if the functioning of the people does not match the level that we see in our hearts. However, we must enter it on a plane parallel to the leaders at the outset of their vision. In other words, we are going where we have been before, only this time on a different plane. Every pastor who has been doing it for some length truly understands the phrase "going where we have been before." How many times have we all felt like where we are is some dejavu experience, or we say "been there, done that" and here we go again. Let's examine ways we can help both us and the people at this particular juncture.

When it comes to design and strategies, I would like to propose that we look at three areas: refining our existing infrastructure, revisiting our training and development components, and releasing people to do the work they are called to do.

REFINING OUR EXISTING INFRASTRUCTURE

One of the first areas we must assess as we try to evaluate the effectiveness of our church organization is that of *__refining our existing infrastructure.__* We must be willing to ask ourselves if our current infrastructure, or underlying foundation, has the capacity to support the vision that we are operating from. If that basic framework of our organization cannot accommodate our vision, then our work is truly cut out for us. It is at this point that we have to now discover if it is a system's problem or a people problem. A system's problem would suggest that we revisit our visions and then translate the visions into identifiable goals. Once we do this, then we must further translate our goals into identifiable tasks that will help us get the job accomplished. Then we must examine our infrastructure and see if the positions or the order of the flow of the operation match the necessary tasks that must be performed in order to get the job done.

For example, in the Keep-A-Gap Church one of the issues that the Calvary group identified is that of "continuing identity with accountability and responsibility." What the group suggested this means is that there is some struggle in the Keep-a-Gap Church with "who is accountable to whom and who is responsible for what." One of the ways in which I would troubleshoot this issue as a consultant would be to first look at the infrastructure and the organizational flow chart. Oops! Did I say organizational flow chart? As quiet as it is kept and as sad as it may seem, the truth of the matter is that there are many churches and organizations that have not designed a clear model as to the flow of leadership and authority. These churches or organizations operate off of assumptions that people will just get it or people know who is who. This in and of itself is an erroneous assumption. As our churches grow and change over time, in terms of the face of the congregation, people seem to know less and less who is responsible for what and who is accountable to whom.

One of the ways to counteract this erroneous assumption and to perpetuate the appropriate knowledge in our local assemblies regarding accountability and responsibility is to create a clear organizational flowchart. Within this flowchart, regardless as to whether it is horizontal or vertical in nature, should be a map delineating clear lines of authority and responsibility. The leader should have this model written so that it can consistently be communicated to the older members who forget and the newer members who do not know. Such communication has the potential to reduce the conflict level within the working relationships of the people.

A second issue that was identified that I think falls in the category of evaluating infrastructure is the issue of "a core group in the church not being reached." The Calvary group suggested that part of the deficit in functioning and operation derives from this fact. Either they are not getting proper information or they are not included in the dissemination of information that will allow them to feel empowered in the church. Another possibility around this is that there could be the assumption that these people understand what is being said from the pulpit or from other leaders regarding the rules and guidelines of the church.

The truth of the matter is that they may be hearing it but not comprehending it in a manner that is conducive to their being able to function in ways which are consistent with that of some of the older members. In order to close the gap and eliminate the division between the new and the old, more emphasis must be placed on the role of continually ministering to the new group in the church. When the organizational chart is examined and the infrastructure is evaluated, where would this task most likely fall and how do we empower those designated to perpetuate information to this unreached core group that will help them be more effective?

REVISIT TRAINING AND DEVELOPMENT

The second thing that we must do in terms of design and strategies is to *revisit the issue of training and development in our churches.* It is my belief that the church is one of the only organizations in our society which takes people into its system and then places them in a position to work while offering them no training. And then we have the gall to expect good results and demand a certain level of output. When we do this to people, we set them up for failure and create the possibility of all sorts of spiritual warfare and havoc in their lives. Simultaneously, we induce potential frustration into the system because now people are functioning who do not know the system's expectations around excellence and who may not know the fundamentals of what is expected of them.

For example, in many of our churches, we assume that because one teaches in the public school system that they will make wonderful Sunday school or Bible school teachers. This assumption is not necessarily true. While the pedagogy may be the same, the content of what we teach in the church is so radically different than our exposure in the secular system that teaching the Bible can be equated to teaching a foreign language. Teaching in the church is foreign to people whose understanding has not been developed and who have not been taught to properly interpret the text. Then, when people stop attending certain classes or get frustrated over the dynamics of our teaching components, we as leaders have the tendency to blame them for their apathy or lack of spiritual appetite.

The issue of training and development is definitely an area that we must give more serious consideration to. For many of us, we merely perpetuate the model we grew up in. Our leaders did not necessarily train us and yet we were effective, so we duplicate this thinking in our own work. Times have changed and the generation we live in is different. People work in a society that is highly technical, and they are accustomed to being trained for whatever work they do. I believe that they bring the expectation of being trained into the church. Thus, they look to be taught or led by trained people and they feel more adept in their functioning when they are trained themselves.

Training is really a simple issue. Firstly, we must assess where people are and be willing to start with them where they are. Secondly, we must show them the vision or the endpoint of what they will be doing and how they need to function. Thirdly, we must be willing to create a way in which development can occur in the difference. This requires investment on behalf of those leaders who have already acquired the skills and the learning necessary to do the work. We must be willing to formally and informally give to the new kid on the block what we have gained over time.

Step Five: *EXECUTION*

RELEASING PEOPLE TO DO THE WORK

The third thing that we should note under this issue of design and strategy is that of releasing people to do the work that they know to do. I put this on the table because it is something that I tend to struggle with most often. As a leader, I am always challenged with the issue of control. The root of the need to control, lies in my own pseudo-perfectionist complex. I call it pseudo because I sometimes expect of people what I do not produce myself. I am quickly coming to grips with the fact that success in ministry is closely correlated with our ability to determine the "ripeness of people," and then being able to release them. When people are ripe and ready, we must trust them to do what they have been trained to do, and to do it well. They will feel empowered when they denote this trust factor and when they understand the confidence that we place in them.

Thus, the execution flows easier because of the investment of time in the people. When people know what to do, they do it better. When trouble arises or people need help getting to the next level of production, intervention is an easier task because persons have learned to function cooperatively. But what happens when, after all of the above investment, there is still trouble in the camp? Where do you turn? Another assumption of this book is that the real issues get solved when both the leaders and the people are examined. Walk with me, then, to the other side of the continuum and let's look at the people.

Let us now examine how to close the gap by revisiting the issues of leadership from a people's perspective. Again, may I reiterate that true leadership will focus simultaneously on the issues from both a leader's perspective, as well as that of the people. The assumption that it is either/or will lead to detrimental consequences with regard to the synergy of the organization or church. Since we have already examined the issues from a pastor's perspective, we must do justice and focus on the followers as it relates to human functioning.

When I was enrolled in the doctoral program at NC State University, I remember one of my professors, who taught a class on Ethnographic Studies, saying that human behavior was basically uncontrollable and unpredictable. This one insight on human behavior has served to really help me diagnose many problems encountered in leadership without being angry or abnormally disturbed with people. On any given day or in any given season of ministry, people can display behaviors that will surprise or sometimes even shock the leader. The truth of the matter is, some of the responses people have towards leadership are legitimate and authentic, while other behaviors are designed for torturing the leader and creating chaos in the congregation. Not everyone, however, would operate under these two extremities. In all reality, most people function the way they do because of learned patterns and prescribed assumptions about life, or a lack of understanding about the current dynamics of leadership. Therefore, we must invest energies around helping people to unlearn these behaviors and to purge their unconscious and subconscious domains of influences stemming from past learning. We also must be willing to answer people's concerns and bring clarity to their struggles so that they will be more willing to follow leadership.

I learned a few years ago, when I was a teacher in the public schools, that people will only respond to our demands as leaders to the degree that they respect our leadership. This respect has to do with both how they perceive we are treating them, as well as their perception of our investment in their lives and their struggles. The following circles capture this dynamic.

RESPECT and
DEMANDS

RESPECT

DEMANDS

What these diagrams suggest is that people will better respond to our demands when our demands are within the scope of their respect for us, for what we do and for the way in which we lead them. If our demands are greater than their respect for us, then we will experience some type of tension in leading. Usually, people will either engage in problematic types of behavior or some mild form of resistance. If they perceive leadership as being open to listen to them, they will make some attempt to explain their resistance or they will subtly try to get the message across. How we troubleshoot problems in our churches or organization that involve people problems is contingent upon the angle from which the problem stems.

For example, Pastor Moses of the Wilderness Church of

Deliverance (Book of Exodus) had a tremendous people problem. His congregation, the Israelites, was basically "dissatisfied with the immediate." When God or Pastor Moses would not respond quickly enough to their needs and complaints, they gravitated towards making the issue a leadership problem. They blamed both God and Moses. Moses had to act with wisdom as to how to handle this church. The first thing that he did was consult with God. On one hand, this was extremely admirable and honorable. After all, God is the Creator and the Sustainer of all life, and it is He that gives us our directives as leaders. However, there were some occasions where God told Moses, "I have already empowered you and have given you instructions, NOW HANDLE IT!" In other words, let these people know that YAHWEH gave you authority to act on His behalf and to govern them.

It did, however, require the wisdom of Moses' father-in-law to reveal to Moses that his organizational chart was wrong. Jethro showed Moses that part of the people problem stemmed from the lack of an organizational structure that would accommodate their needs. Jethro helped Moses institute an Elders' system that would disperse the enormity of the work into smaller and more workable cells. To some degree this eliminated part of the problems the congregation was facing.

So how do we as leaders deal with our problems when they are clearly people issues? Where do we begin in approaching situations that can be scary and at the same time explosive? May I suggest that we use our definition of leadership as a possible approach to this problem? We have suggested that leadership is about "mobilizing the people to do the adaptive work of merging our realities with what we value." The real work here is finding ways to mobilize the people.

Let me propose the following steps as a roadmap for dealing with people issues:

- *CLEARLY*   *Identify the Issue*

- *COLLABORATIVELY*   *Decide on the Adaptive Work*

- *COLLECTIVELY*   *Work on Solving the Problem(s)*

- *CELEBRATE*   *Each Victory Along the Way*

- *CONTINUE*   *To Build Relationship*

In order for us to see how these principles can be used to help bridge the gap in what we desire as leaders and in the current functioning of the people, we will make application of them to the scenario of the Keep-A-Gap Church. Take, for example, the issue of tithing. In the scenario with the Keep-A-Gap Church, it was discovered that only 47 percent of the congregation were tithing regularly and consistently. This means that another 53 percent of the congregation were not tithing at all. We must ask ourselves what does this data tells us.

When I asked the Calvary group this question, they came up with the following possibilities as to what the data suggests as it relates to identifiable issues:

- *Hardness of Heart*

- *Lack of Communication*

- *Private Revelations of the People Vs Congregational Revelation*

- *Personal Beliefs vs Church Beliefs*

- *Relationship Issues as they Relate to God*

- *Lack of Information*

- *Lack of Appreciation for the Church*

- *Personal Situations (people want to pay tithes but they can't)*

- *Church Growth Issue (church grew too fast and people do not understand)*

- *Lack of Understanding of the Vision*

When we view this list, it reveals that the message from the tithing data could be quite diverse. Therefore, it is extremely critical that the church leadership does not try to make decisions based on the data alone. It is necessary, now that they have produced statistical information to support their claim, that the *leadership go to the people to discover the meaning of this data.*

Obviously, we cannot fully explore each of the above issues on the list in the context of this book. Let us therefore choose the issues of "Personal Beliefs versus Church Beliefs" and "Personal Revelations versus Congregational Revelation" as a way to talk about the tithing issue and apply the five steps. These issues suggest that there is a difference between what the church espouses as its belief about tithing and what some of the members espouse as their view. The pastors can stand up on Sunday mornings and quote from the Book of Malachi about robbing God, and some members hear it and still do not embrace it as necessarily being true.

The challenge then for leadership is to determine how to get the value of tithing to become a shared value of the congregation, so that it is no longer just a value of the leaders, but a value of all. A graphic illustration of this is seen below.

CREATE SHARED VALUE

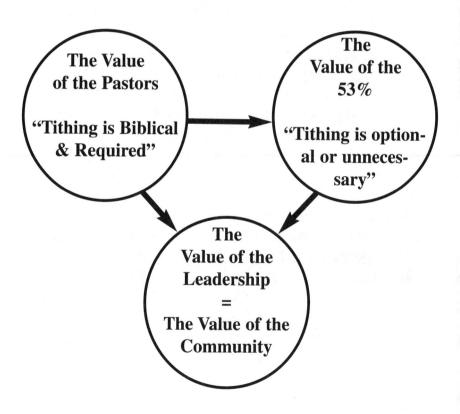

A FIVE STEP APPROACH

1) CLEARLY IDENTIFY THE ISSUE(S)

The first step towards creating a solution that will result in change of behavior and bring forth the desired outcome is to **clearly identify the issue(s).** The question to be answered is, What is the real issue, as stated by the people, at stake, versus the perceived issue, as stated by the pastors and leaders? In order to get to the answer, I recommend a simple **ABC APPROACH.**

*A*lways be attentive and ready to listen. If we, as leaders, are truly going to bring resolve to problems, then we must deem what the people have to say as being important and critical to the context of the issue. Whether we agree or disagree with them is not the focus of this step, but rather creating a means to hear their voice clearly.

*B*e sure that the issue is defined in terms of how the people view the problem versus how the leader defines the problem. It is also important that the issue be stated in a manner that clear action steps can be taken to resolve it.

*C*reate space for people to verbalize their views in an open and free environment that does not involve blaming or shaming.

The leadership must come to acknowledge and recognize that the pulpit message regarding the tithing issue is not as effective as they desire it to be. Therefore, the principle of identifying the issue is key. It is highly possible that the issue of not tithing is only a *SYMPTOMATIC BEHAVIOR* of what the real issue is. The real issue probably has a deeper root, and we must try to get to what that root issue is and not just simply process the manifested behavior.

Therefore, the first step towards this challenge is to *check out assumptions about the behaviors of not paying tithes.* Since we are dealing with 53 percent of the congregation, I would suggest that the church find a way to tap into the thinking of these people. Perhaps small group consultations would be possible or one-on-one surveys. There must be some means of getting to the people and engaging them in conversations regarding what the reasons might be as to why they are not paying tithes. I know that we think this is ridiculous because people should automatically love God and respect the word of God enough that they just obey what we say. We may discover some hidden information that could unlock this behavior and cause a tremendous increase in the tithing patterns of our churches.

Checking out assumptions will require us to listen and to hear what people are saying. As the Calvary group suggested, one assumption is that there is some difference in the perspectives on tithing. If we check this out with the people and discover this to be true, then we must subsequently create strategies to address these perspectives.

2)   COLLABORATIVELY DECIDE ON THE ADAPTIVE WORK

As we devise strategies for creating a proper perspective on tithing, it is vital to the longevity of what we create that the people are involved in the process of identifying the adaptive work necessary. Part of the work will require teaching about tithing from both a biblical and a practical perspective. I suspect that one dimension of this challenge lies in the people's view of the Bible as the infallible word of God. We live in a time when people do not necessarily see the Bible as the previous generation did. When we, the older generation, were told what the Bible says to do about anything, there was such reverence and fear in our hearts that we did it.

Times are different now. We can say that the Bible says do so and so, and this generation does not necessarily buy into this mode of conformity to the word. This generation needs to be taught in more intimate settings. They need to consider the issue from an intellectual perspective and a school book approach. They also need to know the benefits of tithing and how it will truly make a difference in their lives. I am not sure we can effectively convey all of this from the pulpit and simultaneously involve them in a way in which they can raise questions. Therefore, we must be willing to solicit their help in creating a way to encourage more in the congregation to be committed to tithing. We must ask them what their approach towards solving this gap would be.

SOME SUGGESTED IDEAS FOR THE ADAPTIVE WORK

TEACHING
- Educate People – people transitioning out of the world do not understand the Tithing Principle

• Teach Money Management and/or Debt
Reduction Strategies

LEADERSHIP MODELING PAYING TITHES
• We, as leaders, must practice what we preach.
Do it openly so that the people will see

INCLUSIVENESS
• Share benefits of paying tithes on a personal
basis
• Show congregation how they are included in
God's thoughts on tithing through the Word

GO IN THE MIDST OF THE PEOPLE
• Have members share real life challenges as
they struggled with the issue

TOUCH PEOPLE WHERE THEY ARE
• Acknowledge the reality in their circumstances and situations while simultaneously
challenging them to trust God

3) *COLLECTIVELY WORK ON SOLVING THE
PROBLEM*

After we collaboratively decide on ways to bridge the gap in
the tithing issue, we must then not be afraid to allow those
who are in the 53 percent to participate in the process of solving the problem. Perhaps we could use techniques such as
"each one reach one" or small study groups or home visitations. I believe that there would be synergy created when all

are working on the issue together.

Some suggested ideas:

- Sunday Morning Sermons on Tithing
- Bible Study lessons on Tithing with space for questions/answers
- One-on-One Involvement: designate key people to individually touch people where they are through visitations, conversations, etc.
- Small Groups
- Deal with the Spiritual Implication: the underlying implication of this behavior is that there is a spiritual problem. Encourage more effective prayer lives, more involvement in the Word and Word study, enhancing relationship with God and intimacy towards the church

4) CELEBRATE EACH VICTORY ALONG THE WAY

An important dimension of this work is for us to learn to celebrate along the way. I am convinced that this is something the church does not do enough of on a consistent basis. As we experience change in behaviors and shifts in thinking patterns, we must use these successful experiences to generate change and shifts in the larger. Learning to report back to the people that the percentage in tithing has increased to 60 percent is important. At this point, we must start to focus on the increase rather than being so angry at the deficit that we forget to celebrate what is happening.

5)   *CONTINUE TO BUILD RELATIONSHIPS*

Once we have generated successes and created energy within the congregation, we must continue to foster it within our people. Many of the people probably now pay tithes not only because they were taught differently, but also because they were given interaction with others, along with special attention. In other words, the people respond to relationship building just like they do to the word of the Lord. As a matter of fact, people are more apt to give of their finances when they sense some kind of personal touch emanating from leadership. When people feel respected and have significance, it is easier for them to give of their possessions. We, as leaders, must capitalize on this understanding without feeling as if this is sacrilegious or beneath the scope of our work.

I would suggest that you as a reader and a leader take some of the other issues identified in the above list and work through ways to bring resolve. Try using the five principles suggested. Tremendous learning can stem from this type of engagement.

I realize that I could go on and on because this subject is dear to my heart and I know that the issue of leadership is something that we must learn to wrestle with and embrace in the church of God. So my prayer is that you will continue to pursue the heart of God in order that you might more effectively lead his people and discover ways to bring the people closer to your heart. Together, we can make a difference in the kingdom of God.

———Chapter 7———
The Next Generation

Recently, a group called Mary and Mary emerged on the music scene. They rapidly and overwhelmingly took the hearts of the young people by storm. I observed my fifteen-year-old daughter become almost mesmerized and totally fascinated by this group. Every time they would come on the radio she would say, "Daddy, turn that up. That's Mary and Mary!" I would turn the radio up and listen to the movement of the songs. Initially, it sounded like another Rhythm and Blues artist with a crossover appeal to the younger generation of believers. Then, when she insisted that I buy her the CD, I finally sat down with her and listened to the entire CD. I was amazed as to what I discovered. This contemporary group was singing many of the same songs that I used to listen to by such reputable artists as Rev. James Cleveland. Their rendition and rearrangement of his song "I Don't Feel No Ways Tired" absolutely blessed my soul, and I found myself gravitating to the rendition of Mary and Mary as opposed to that of the Rev. James Cleveland. I also went out and bought my own personal copy of the CD so that I would not have to compete with my daughter, who guarded hers as if it were pure gold. I found myself listening to my CD every day and every time I got into the car.

As I reflected over this scenario, I came to realize that inherent in this interaction with my daughter was some message about how the church must come to grips with ways in which it must reach and minister to the next generation. I gained insights about the dynamic of the next generation that is quite phenomenal in terms of what moves this generation and what it wants. Thus, I concluded that only when the church takes the challenge of ministering to the next generation seriously, will it truly have an impact on the lives of this upcoming generation. The next generation is not necessarily rebelling against our message, but rather they are challenging our methods in terms of delivery of the message itself. In my mind, this is congruent with an eternal and progressive God, who is interested in the preservation of the Gospel while ministering to every generation, from the first man Adam to our latest generation "Y." The Bible itself, even though it is a book that is historic and old, still has the power to reach and minister to a young generation that needs to hear its message. It will be our ability to make the word relevant that will bring this book to life for the young.

So the question becomes, How do we, the church, bridge the gap between the different generations that co-exist within our walls? How do we give authenticity, respectability and validity to each generation and at the same time, perpetuate the message of the word of the Lord without compromise? How do we become cringe-free and totally relevant to the diversity of generations, while simultaneously not compromising our core beliefs? How do we change our methods and not feel some sense of loss of what is important, but rather a sense of gaining what is most valuable? Our challenges are ahead of us, and we must plunge deep into the waters if we are going to effectively win a new generation for Christ and cause them to know God intimately. I invite you to walk with me through this chapter as we discuss this topic a little more in depth.

By now you probably realize that I like to give a roadmap of where we are going before we start on the journey. In this last chapter, the map looks like this: firstly, we must revisit the MAKE-UP of our congregations in order to gain a comprehensive view of our targeted groups within and without the church. This will help determine the way in which we go about doing ministry. Secondly, we will try to reveal the MINDSETS of the diverse generations within the church. Only when we are aware as to what is important to each generation and what they think about can we determine what will be effective with the generations. Thirdly, we will work on MASTERING our fears and feelings about the diverse groups, as well as about working together in collaborative ways to produce excellence in ministry for the total population of the church. Fourthly, we will explore METHODOLOGIES that are useful in redefining and reengaging ways in which we do ministry. Finally, we will discover what we need as an older generation, to MOVE OVER SOME so that there will be plenty of room for all in God's church.

MAKE-UP OF THE CHURCH

When we look at the twenty-first century church, we see a clear and powerful composition of diverse groups within the church walls. It seems to me that the aim of the Gospel, which is to compel people to come from all walks of life, is being fulfilled in many of our churches. We can now look at congregations and see a true mixing pot of the old and the young, the rich and the poor, the black and the white, the Asian and the Hispanic, and the Traditionalist and the Non-traditionalist, etc. What is most interesting is that there is a large cross section of generation mixtures in the church. We have the older generation, who now are approximately sixty to eighty plus years, and the baby boomers, who emerged from World War 2. Then there is Generation X, who are the children of the baby boomers and who are quite affluent and educated. Finally, there is Generation Y, who is known for its hip-hop ways and technological norms.

Along with this cultural and generational diversity, we also see an anointing sweeping across the churches of America to bring blessings and fresh healing oil to each of these groups. Yet we look at some churches that embrace this mixture and movement, while other churches resist mightily this occurrence within its walls. Why do some churches embrace and welcome this move, while others decree it to be a compromise of the standards of God and of holiness?

I am convinced that the pastors and leaders who want to be relevant in our ministries are carefully engaging in the process of understanding the current make-up of growing churches in America, while simultaneously focusing on dissecting the make-up of our own local assemblies. We are coming to believe that diversity is important and is to be valued. For many of us, there is clear generation diversity and we value what each generation brings to the table.

We have the elderly and the elders, who founded the church. Many of these people gave birth to local assemblies with their sweat, blood, tears and labor. For many of these people, the church represents their place of financial investment amid the scarcity of resources that they did have. Yet they believed in giving to God's church. To many of them, the old hymns of the church have a place of utmost respect and are not to be compromised. Songs like "The Lord Will Make a Way Somehow" or "Hold to God's Unchanging Hand" must be sung just like they are in the hymn book in order for the church to grasp the full significance of their meaning. The power of these songs lies in the experiential nature of the words to the lives of these soldiers for the Lord.

When the Baby Boomers came to the table, they brought fresh management styles and new leadership ideologies to the church. They have quickly become the generation to now manage the church due to their education, finances and exposure to corporate America. In many ways, this group has managed to perpetuate some of the ways and means of the elders, while simultaneously shifting the church to a greater degree of sophistication in its operation. Many of the elderly are proud of their sons and daughters carrying on the work of the church, as well as being proud of the ways in which they have enhanced and enlarged the scope of ministry through diverse programs and advanced systems of operation.

But what about Generation X, whose emphasis is on changing fads and changing trends? This generation seems so technologically oriented that they are more interested in seeing God on a Web site versus experiencing him in the hymn book. What do we do with a Generation X who wants to understand tithing from an investment perspective versus just sheer obedience to Malachi 3:8? What about this Generation X who majors in understanding the Bible from different translations of it versus just being happy with the King James Version? What do they bring to the table? In its quest to discover this answer, the church has to come to appreciate the ways in which it has become more computer literate, more technologically astute, and more competent in advertising and promoting the church.

And then there is the Generation Y. We define them as the hip-hop generation, whose beat to music is more in sync to rapping those hymns than singing them from the hymn book. How does the church work with a generation of people whose pants hang down, whose hair is braided, and who talks in a language that is hardly translatable to the elderly? This generation could easily have Cyberspace Church, could take the songs of the church and change their beat and alter the words. This group often views the church as one of many possible options to explore their spirituality. How do we come to know what they bring to the table, and how do we work cooperatively with them to gain the essence of who they are? Herein lies the struggle to bridge the gap and the matter by which I continue to write.

The challenge for the church is clear. In light of all these diverse generations within the church, it must discover ways to effectively reach each of these groups. It must preserve its history, while simultaneously perpetuating its future. The idea of Preservation versus Perpetuation is rooted within the different generations. I am convinced that it will be the older generation and the Baby Boomers that will focus on preserving the church's history, but I believe it will be Generation X and Generation Y that will perpetuate the life of the church and our future understanding of our religion. Therefore, we must take the time to determine how to effectively reach this generation and cooperatively bring the church to its desired end.

The changing of the guards or the releasing of the church into the hands of the next generation reminds me of the story of Israel. According to the Book of Numbers, the generation that went into the wilderness was not the same generation that came out of the wilderness. All those who went into the wilderness from Egypt died in the wilderness for various reasons: some of which are the spirits of complaining and murmuring and constant rebellion. The generation that came out of the wilderness were the children of the elders of Israel that went into the wilderness. It was this new generation that had to learn and come to know the heart of God in a way that they could perpetuate the history of the Jewish people and simultaneously relay the heart of God to others. Joshua had to foster methods and techniques to teach this generation about God—while he was in his prime. The truth is that Joshua would die, and who then would carry out the purposes of Yahweh? Joshua knew it would be the next generation. Thus, God required that this new generation be circumcised so that they would be connected to the historical covenant enough to perpetuate it, as they sought to discover their own ways to worship God.

To me, this is the challenge in bridging the gap between the generations. We must find ways to perpetuate history and preserve the tenets of the faith, while giving way to forms and methods that are relevant to the thinking and the understanding of our contemporary generations.

MINDSETS OF NEW GENERATIONS

One of the things that the young people will quickly tell us older people is that they do not want to sit through another church service and listen to old hymns, a bunch of litanies and the preacher talk about Peter, James and John. So if the younger generation does not want this, what then do they want? I believe that this new generation is sending a strong message out to the church saying, "If you want to reach us and get to know us, then you must first make strides to understand our worldview." The worldview of Generation X and Generation Y are certainly different than those of the previous generations. This new generation no longer has it hard like we did. Preaching about how we used to work in the tobacco field and find God in the wet dew is not attractive to this generation. Telling about how we saw the stars at night and the ground at the same time because of the conditions of our homes no longer carry a message that will cause this generation to know God.

Yet and still, many of their challenges are analogous and parallel to our own experiences. Thus, we must take the same Word and the same Bible that brought us out of the dungeons and dunghill, and find a way to present it to them so that they will see themselves. The only way we can do this is to make efforts to understand their worldviews. A person's worldview consists of the paradigm by which that person interprets the world around him or her as they have come to know it, based upon his or her culture, experiences, and exposure. Many of the generations after us have come to interpret their world through a larger lens than the one our generation used.

In my day, most of the world, from my perspective and geographical place, was mainly black and white. This is true literally and figuratively. Literally, I grew up in an environment at home and at church that had only two extremes, a black world and a white world. The black people did their thing, and the white people did their's. Figuratively speaking, most ideas and moral struggles where primarily black and white. Either it was wrong or it was right. If you did not know, the church would explain it to you.

Today, the world is filled with many colors and races of people, and they all dwell in the same geographical space. Therefore, this new generation has a broader view of what God means by "all nations are one" or "in Christ, there is neither Jew nor Greek, male nor female, bond nor free." Likewise, the multiplicity of ideas and morals has to be contended with by this generation. There is no longer a mere black and white issue on many of the moral standards that the church once deemed as clear. Even as we ascend to a place of establishing standards and encouraging this generation to take a stand, we must be able to identify with the entourage of ideas that they hear on a daily basis. In addition to this, we must be able to identify with the ways in which this creates a greater complexity about many of the issues.

From a comparative perspective, this new generation has a lot more to contend with than many of us who are older. Besides the quantity of dealing, they also have adopted a different approach to life than what we did. I think my generation prided itself on being personal and intimate with the church and the saints. In many ways, we were taught to "wait on the Lord" and to some degree embrace passivity. Passivity was considered more divine than aggressiveness. This new generation, however, is more radical in nature and more global in scope. They see an aggressive society on a daily basis, and they have come to understand that they must function likewise if they are going to remain competitive. They have brought this energy into the church. In many ways, they are more in line with kingdom thinking than the older generation. The Scripture declares that the kingdom of God suffers violence and the violent must take it by force (Matthew 11:12). This Scripture could easily be the adopted motto of this new generation of young people as they pursue life from such an aggressive approach.

MASTER OUR FEARS AND FEELINGS

Such aggression brings fear to the older generation around what will be the outcome of a generation who seems to make decisions and do things so swiftly without consulting God. If you can remember, at the outset of the book I suggested that we focus on several dimensions of what causes people to do what they do. I proposed that we examine the cognitive, the behavioral and the emotional dimensions. Is our fear of how this new generation operates and of what we might lose getting in the way of our ability to deal across generations, embracing what they need? As leaders and pastors, we must deal with our fears. We must determine ways in which our feelings play into the need to either control the dynamics of what happens with the next generation or get in the way of our ability to release them into the fullness of their experience in the church.

In order to facilitate our release of this next generation, we should start with a simple reality check. The truth of the matter is that it will be the next generation that will carry on the work of the ministry. Time and biology will attest to this truth.

Therefore, we must overcome our fears and allow ourselves to go through the grieving process of feeling sad about losing those traditions that are dear to us. The irony of this dynamic is that if we would take the time to get into the hearts and minds of the next generation, we will gain more by being with them than by staying away from them. We will consciously and subconsciously pass on our ideas and our heritage. We will discover that this generation is not afraid of us, and that all they really want is to be validated by us and to be challenged in ways that are relevant to their own experiences. I believe that within them is the capacity to translate our traditions into a new language that will be theirs, while it will simultaneously contain remnants of the old. What a joyful time this will be when we see this happening in a ubiquitous fashion with Christendom. How do we successfully bridge the gap?

METHODOLOGIES

In order to make this happen, we must challenge our methods of doing what we do. We must change and be willing to do things differently. I am offering a few suggestions that I believe could make a difference in bridging the gap between generations.

- WE MUST ***"Love more than we Hate."***

We, as pastors and leaders, have to possess an overwhelming love for the next generation that flows out of the heart of God.

When we love according to the Scripture, we will want the best for this generation. We will deem and esteem them higher than ourselves, and thus we will create ministry for them that will meet their needs and not ours. When our hate for the things they do become a cloud over who they are, we cannot effectively lead nor minister to them. Both the next generation, as well as we, will become frustrated. They will sense our fear of them and our hate for their ploys, their tactics, their need for loud music and liveliness in worship. When they sense our hate, they will become radical and rebellious and, thus, cause friction among us. Eventually, they will leave our assemblies and find a church that will embrace and accept them and their culture. When we love them, they are free. Out of freedom flows creativity and ways to be.

• WE MUST BE WILLING TO *"Listen more than we Talk."*

We must listen to the language and linguistics of the next generation. As they talk, they will give us clues as to how to comprehend their world. They will translate their language for us, and we will soon be able to speak their language and talk their talk. We cannot be afraid of this. This will demand that we work together in collaborative ways to foster the vision and to promote the heartbeat of the pastor and/or leaders. We must embrace inclusiveness. This will require the leaders to unveil the vision to the next generation and then listen as they translate it into their language and their world. When they emerge with ideas and suggestions, we must be willing to include them and deem them as valuable and relevant.

- WE MUST *"Let them Be Who They Are."*

This is so important. Just let them be who they are and allow them to become teachers to the elderly. They will teach us their skills, train us on the Internet, show us their music, and make our churches more global in perspective. They will help us get in step with their beat and march to their drummer.

- WE MUST *"Learn rather than Assume."*

They will try to tell us the ways in which their stuff is different than ours. Sometimes, we have a closed mind and declare that it is all the same. As a result, we operate out of assumptions about them and about what they want and need. This only gets in the way. When we, as leaders, get in a learning posture, we will hear them and then find ways to match the magnitude of their plights.

When we look at what is happening in society, we see that many of the problems of this generation are similar to those of other generations. What is different is the magnitude and the scope of the problem. For example, almost every generation has had to contend with drugs. It is, however, this generation that seems to have to struggle with it in a magnanimity that far exceeds any of the previous generations. How, then, do we make effective a message and a Gospel that addresses this issue in a way that the church is effective in helping this generation contend with a problem that could virtually cause them to become extinct? May I reiterate, if we learn from them, they will teach us.

- FINALLY, WE MUST *"Loosen our Grip and Move Over Some."*

We must be willing to make room for them in such a way that they feel invited to the table. Some of us must be willing to let go of positions that we have held for years and years, while some of us must learn to do things another way. An example of this is for us as older preachers, to challenge ourselves around our diversity in preaching style. Hooping and hollering for one hour is difficult for this new generation to digest. We must make our sermons more relevant in ways that this new congregation identifies with, as well as vary our delivery techniques to be inclusive of ways in which this new generation receives the word. We must be willing to move over a little and do things differently.

Of course, all of the above suggestions are one-sided and will only be effective if there is reciprocity stemming from the new generation. The new generation must grasp the need to be openminded and understanding of the older generation. Generation X and Generation Y cannot take their degrees and education, or their wealth and influence and dismiss the older generation as being ignorant and unlearned. This will only result in exacerbated gaps between the two. Rather, they must become as generation sensitive as the older and work to discover ways to send positive energy to the older generation. When both are synchronized, there will emerge a synergy that will cause the church to prosper and that will represent the heartbeat of the leader.

Bibliography

Barna, George. *The Power of Vision.* Ventura, California: Regal Books (1992).

Heifetz, Ronald A. *Leadership Without Easy Answers.* Cambridge, Massachusetts: The Belknap Press of Harvard University Press (1994).

Maxwell, John C. *Developing The Leader Within You.* Nashville: Thomas Nelson Publishers (1993).

V.I.S.I.O.N.S., Vigorous Interventions in Ongoing Natural Settings. Massachusetts: Boston.

Wheatley, Margaret. *A Simpler Way.* Berkeley, California: Berrett-Koehler Publishers (1996).